The Dutch in the Americas

Sponsors

ING BARINGS

THE EQUITABLE GALLERY OF THE
EQUITABLE LIFE ASSURANCE SOCIETY

Benefactors

ACORN FOUNDATION

SCHIPHOL USA

SOCIETY OF THE DAUGHTERS OF HOLLAND DAMES

Patrons Committee

H.E. ADRIAAN JACOBOVITS DE SZEGED,
AMBASSADOR OF THE NETHERLANDS TO THE UNITED STATES,
HONORARY PATRON

MRS. JAMES VAN ALEN, *CHAIRWOMAN*

THE HONORABLE J. WILLIAM MIDDENDORF, II, *CHAIRMAN*

MR. J. CARTER BROWN

MR. JAN FLINTERMAN

MR. AND MRS. HOUGHTON P. METCALF, JR.

MRS. DANIEL OLIVER

MR. ROBERT S. PIRIE

MRS. ALEXANDER O. VIETOR

MR. AND MRS. WILLIAM B. WARREN

Patrons

MR. AND MRS. THOMAS R. ADAMS

MR. AND MRS. RUSSELL B. AITKEN

AKZO NOBEL

MRS. VINCENT ASTOR

GREGORY AND LISA BARNHILL

MR. AND MRS. BERNARD E. BELL

MR. LYMAN G. BLOOMINGDALE

KATHRYN BRINCKERHOFF AND
THOMAS SLATTERY

MR. AND MRS. T. KIMBALL BROOKER

MR. AND MRS. DOUGLAS W. BROWN

THOMAS AND ANTONIA BRYSON

LINDA AND VINCENT BUONANNO

MR. JAMES H. CAREY

MR. AND MRS. FINN M. W. CASPERSEN

DR. AND MRS. ALFREDO C. CASSIET

MRS. MARION O. CHARLES

CITCO CORPORATE SERVICES, INC.,
IN MEMORY OF A.A.G. SMEETS

MR. AND MRS. MAURITS EDERSHEIM

MR. AND MRS. GEORGE D. EDWARDS, JR.

LINCOLN AND RUTH B. EKSTROM

ELSEVIER SCIENCE, INC.

AMBASSADOR AND MRS. EDWARD E. ELSON

MR. AND MRS. JOSÉ A. ESTEVE

MRS. ANGELA B. FISCHER

MR. AND MRS. MICHAEL FOLEY / HEINEKEN USA

MR. AND MRS. TIMOTHY C. FORBES

MR. PETER H. B. FRELINGHUYSEN

MR. HELMUT N. FRIEDLAENDER

DR. PAUL WILLIAM GARBER

MR. ROBERT B. GLYNN

MR. ROBERT N. GORDON

MR. PETER GREEN

MR. AND MRS. REINALDO HERRERA

MR. AND MRS. WOLFGANG A. HERZ

ROBERTA AND RICHARD HUBER

MR. AND MRS. JEROME KAMERMAN

KPN US

MR. NORMAN B. LEVENTHAL

MR. AND MRS. STANLEY LIVINGSTON, JR.

MR. GUY LOMBARDO

MR. AND MRS. CALEB LORING, JR.

MR. VINCENT M. LOVE

MR. AND MRS. GEORGE LOWRY

MR. AND MRS. NICHOLAS S. LUDINGTON, JR.

MARTAYAN LAN RARE BOOKS AND MAPS

MR. AND MRS. PAUL MELLON

MR. HENRY MIDDENDORF

THE NETHERLAND-AMERICA FOUNDATION

MR. AND MRS. JEAN R. PERRETTE

RABOBANK NEDERLAND

MR. AND MRS. RICHARD C. RAMER

MR. WILLIAM S. REESE

RORY RIGGS AND JEREMY FITZGERALD

MR. MORDECAI ROSENFELD

JAMES AND MARY ELLEN RUDOLPH

MR. DONALD L. SAUNDERS

MR. TIMOTHY R. SCHANTZ

CAROLINE F. AND STUART B. SCHIMMEL

MR. AND MRS. STANLEY DEFOREST SCOTT

MR. AND MRS. ROBERT SESSLER

MR. AND MRS. ROBERT B. SHEA

ANN M. SHORIN

MR. AND MRS. CLINTON I. SMULLYAN, JR.

MR. AND MRS. FRANK S. STREETER

MR. CHARLES J. TANENBAUM

MR. AND MRS. GUSTAVO A. TAVARES

MR. AND MRS. J. THOMAS TOUCHTON

MR. THOMAS M. VALENZUELA

MR. AND MRS. JAMES L. VAN ALEN, II

MR. AND MRS. WILLIAM L. VAN ALEN, JR.

MR. AND MRS. JOHN A. VAN BEUREN

THE HON. TJACO VAN DEN HOUT

EDITH AND LOET VELMANS

MR. AND MRS. WILLIAM A. VIALL

MR. FRANZ VON ZIEGESAR

PATRICIA AND CHARLES WATTS

MR. AND MRS. A. O. WAY

MR. AND MRS. JOHN HAZEN WHITE, SR.

DR. AND MRS. J. ALLEN YAGER

ITINERARIO,

Voyage ofte Schipvaert / van Jan Huygen van Linschoten naer Oost ofte Portugaels In-

dien / inhoudende een corte beschrijvinghe der selver Landen ende Zee-custen / met aen-
wijsinge van alle de voornaemde principale Havens / Revieren / hoecken ende plaetsen / tot noch
toe vande Portugesen ontdeckt ende bekent: Waer by ghevoeght zijn / niet alleen die Conterfeytsels vande habijten / drachten ende wesen / so vande Portugesen aldaer residerende / als vande ingeboornen Indianen / ende huere Tempels / Afgoden / Huysinge / met die voornaemste
Boomen / Vruchten / kruyden / Specerijen / ende diergelijcke materialen / als ooc die
manieren des selfden Volckes / so in hunnen Godts-diensten / als in Politie
en Huijs-houdinghe: maer ooc een corte verhalinge van de Coophan-
delingen / hoe en waer die ghedreven en ghevonden worden /
met die ghedenckweerdichste geschiedenissen /
voorghevallen den tijt zijnder
residentie aldaer.

Alles beschreven ende by een vergadert, door den selfden, seer nut, oorbaer,
ende oock vermakelijcken voor alle curieuse ende Lief-
hebbers van vreemdigheden.

t'AMSTELREDAM.

By Cornelis Claesz. op't VVater, in't Schrijf-boeck, by de oude Brugghe.
Anno CIƆ. IƆ. XCVI.

FRONTISPIECE   The title-page of Linschoten's *Itinerario* (Amsterdam, 1596), featuring
four ports of the Netherlands: Antwerp, Amsterdam, Middelburg, and Enkhuizen.

The Dutch in the Americas

1600-1800

by WIM KLOOSTER

A Narrative History

with the Catalogue of an Exhibition of

Rare Prints, Maps, and Illustrated Books

from the John Carter Brown Library

The John Carter Brown Library

Providence, Rhode Island

1997

EXHIBITION SITES

The John Carter Brown Library

Providence, Rhode Island

May 9 to September 15, 1997

The Equitable Gallery

New York, New York

January 22 to April 4, 1998

Correspondence should be directed to:
The John Carter Brown Library
Box 1894
Providence, Rhode Island 02912

The John Carter Brown Library is an independently
funded and administered institution for advanced research
in history and the humanities at Brown University

ISBN 0-916617-50-5 CLOTH
ISBN 0-916617-51-3 PAPER

Contents

List of Illustrations

List of Color Plates

List of Maps

Preface

The beginnings of the John Carter Brown Library project on the Dutch in the Americas go back to a casual remark I made to Mrs. Alexander Vietor about the excellence of the Library's collection of Dutch materials. Ever alert to project possibilities that might contribute to better public understanding of the past, Mrs. Vietor in a matter of weeks had arranged a luncheon for us with the Consul-General of the Netherlands in New York, the outcome of which was that the Library agreed to organize an exhibition featuring our Dutch collection.

The JCB collection on the Dutch empire and its commercial and military activities in the Western Hemisphere before ca. 1800 is excellent, but it is also little known and little used. Hence, we had a natural interest in the mounting of an exhibition and the production of an exhibition catalogue that would help to publicize these holdings—limited though use of the materials would always be because of the prevailing unfamiliarity in this country with the Dutch language. But our assent to this undertaking would never have been so readily granted had there not been opportunely in residence at the JCB at the time a young Dutch scholar making use of the collection who seemed to us to have all of the equipment required to carry such a project forward.

This was Wim Klooster, a JCB research fellow, who agreed to divert time from his own personal research on European mercantilism and Dutch smuggling to work instead on the task of surveying thousands of titles in the Library, in five or six different languages, and culling from this overview about 175 items for an exhibition. Beyond that chore, we asked Dr. Klooster also to write, in English, a short narrative history on the Dutch ventures in the West during the colonial period.

The difficulty of organizing this information into a short book can be gauged by the fact that there is no pre-existing work that attempts such a synthesis. There are books on the Dutch in Suriname and the Wild Coast, and books on the Dutch in New York and in Brazil, and dozens of specialized studies touching on this matter or that relating to the involvement of the Netherlands in the Americas, but no single work that attempts to integrate into a coherent story the different facets of the extraordinary Dutch expansion to the West—as distinguished from the better known and better studied history of Dutch expansion to the East, to South Africa, Indonesia, and Japan, where the Dutch presence was far more prominent and longer-lived.

Wim Klooster remained at the JCB for two years, with support from various sources, including the

Acorn Foundation, the Fulbright Program, the Dutch government, and Library fellowship funds, part of the time progressing with his own projects and part of the time preparing the text of the exhibition catalogue, which he produced on schedule and in splendid order.

Such projects, of course, are also necessarily team efforts. Mr. Burton Van Name Edwards, a rare book cataloguer on the permanent JCB staff, organized all of the book citations in the exhibition and the catalogue into systematic and proper cataloguer's format, a process that involves a close examination of the bibliographical characteristics of each title. The core of his work is evident in the bibliography section at the end of the catalogue. Mr. Klooster's text was read in manuscript by Patricia Bonomi of New York University, Pieter Emmer of the University of Leiden, and James Tanis of Bryn Mawr College, all of whom offered valuable suggestions for improvement.

We also called upon the various skills and expertise of other JCB staff members. To cite any person's help is possibly to do injustice to the contributions of others. However, I do want to acknowledge here in particular the editorial contributions of Dennis C. Landis, Curator of European Books, and the assistance also of Susan Danforth, Curator of Maps and Prints, who has been the principal person in converting the narrative of the exhibition catalogue into the text or script of the exhibition itself. It is a pleasure to note here, too, that all of the illustrations in the volume were originally shot by Richard Hurley, the Library's photographer.

The modern maps were drawn by Alex Tait of Equator Graphics in Washington, D.C.

At an early stage, when we were still conceptualizing the project, I benefited from a useful conversation with Mr. Hendrik Edelman, and various officers in the Dutch Consulate in New York at the time—Mr. Tjaco van den Hout, the Consul General; Mr. Frank Ligtvoet; and Mr. Henry Kol—were also of great assistance.

The Consulate, Mrs. Vietor, and the Netherland-America Foundation at the very beginning offered the Library the seed money needed to get the project underway, and the Library subsequently was the beneficiary of numerous gifts from generous Benefactors and Patrons, all of whom are recognized on the preceding pages. We wish to thank in particular the members of the Patrons Committee, and His Excellency Adriaan Jacobovits de Szeged, formerly Ambassador of the Netherlands to the United States, who lent their names and prestige to the project.

The essential major funding for the exhibition and the catalogue were granted to the Library by ING Barings and by the Equitable Gallery, our esteemed Sponsors. The Gallery has been a close partner from the beginning as well as a financial Sponsor, and much of what we have been able to accomplish is owed to its support.

Of all the great New World colonial empires, the Spanish, the Portuguese, the French, the Dutch, and the English, each with their striking particularities, that created by the Netherlands is the least generally known and understood. The story is one that may be said to be full of improbabilities if not for the fact that the entire early modern era of Europe—let us say, the period between 1400 and 1800—in its overseas adventures is amazing and improbable.

If the past century is one that dazzles by its technological miracles, the early modern period seems most striking above all for episode after episode of sheer human pluck and audacity. The feats of men on land and sea carried out over staggering distances, with the help only of a handicraft technology of wood and iron, seem so tremendous that one wonders if it is the same human race as our own that could try and endure so much.

The scope of what happened in the Americas was unprecedented: the effort to exert political control over millions of square miles of populated territory; the forced migration and enslavement of millions of African laborers; the voluntary emigration of tens of thousands of Europeans; the encounter throughout the hemisphere with millions of indigenous peoples whose cultures were totally alien to European experience; the production of new wealth in the form of gold and silver, fish, fur, and lumber, and sugar and tobacco that dwarfed all prior human imaginings.

In all of this process the Netherlands, a small country of under two million people in the seventeenth century and with a territory of some 14,000 square miles, were not only major participants but also outstanding documentors and recorders. That ultimately the Netherlanders' ambitions in the West exceeded their capability as a colonial power, which is the story told herein, did not impair the country's production of texts and pictures that can illuminate for us the past of the Americas. With the exception of a few Caribbean outposts, the Dutch were largely driven out, but they left a lasting legacy in many forms.

Countless examples could be cited of Dutch influence and inspiration through the centuries. One instance is Captain John Smith, a leader in the English colonization of Virginia, who struggled to hold up the Dutch example on the matter of where American wealth was to be found. Three-hundred-

and-eighty years ago, in 1616, Smith had prescient advice for the English, writing specifically about the potential of New England for economic growth.

Stop dreaming about finding gold and silver, Smith said, "the maine Staple" for the development of New England should be "fish; which however it may seeme a mean and a base commoditie, yet who will but truely take the pains and consider the sequell, I thinke will allow it well worth the labour. . . . Who doth not know that the poore Hollanders, chiefly by fishing, at a great charge and labour in all weathers in the open Sea, are made a people so hardy, and industrious? and by the venting this poor commodity to Easterlings [i.e., the Baltic coast] for . . . Wood, Flax, Pitch, Tarre, Rosin, Cordage and such like (which they exchange againe, to the French, Spaniards, Portugales, and English, etc.) . . . are made so mighty, strong and rich, as no State but Venice, of twice their magnitude, is so well furnished with so many faire Cities, goodly Townes, strong Fortresses, and that aboundance of shipping and all sorts of marchandize, as well of Golde, Silver, Pearles, Diamonds, Pretious stones, Silkes, Velvets, and Cloth of Golde."

"What Voyages and Discoveries, East and West, North and South, yea about the world, make they?" Smith continued. "What an Army by Sea and Land, have they long maintained in despite of one of the greatest Princes of the World? And never could the Spaniard with all his Mynes of golde and Silver, pay his debts, his friends, and army, halfe so truly, as the Hollanders stil have done by this contemptible trade of fish. Divers (I know) may alledge many other assistances: But this is their Myne; and the Sea the source of those silvered streames of all their vertue; which hath made them now the very miracle of industrie, the pattern of perfection for these affaires."

When the John Carter Brown Library assembles an exhibition of this size, and produces a catalogue, we have several goals in mind. There is, of course, the desire to contribute to public education concerning the history of this hemisphere, which increasingly is an integrated if not united part of the globe. But we wish also specifically to publicize the strength of the holdings of the Library in special areas, such as Dutch colonial history, as a means of encouraging scholars to make use of this material. Hence, as in the case of all JCB exhibitions, all of the material referred to in this catalogue, and virtually all of the material in the exhibition at the Equitable Gallery, is from this Library alone. For the exhibition we borrowed only a dozen or so non-textual works—paintings, furniture, silver—simply as an enhancement to the printed and manuscript items.

To put on an exhibition on a subject so vast as the Dutch in the Americas, drawing only upon what is in the John Carter Brown Library, incurs some risks that the subject will be scantily treated, with many visible holes in what is represented. That is a risk indeed, but the Library has been collecting original materials on this subject for 150 years, and we trust the ground has been well covered concerning a narrative that stretches from Hudson Bay to Tierra del Fuego.

The Chronological Bibliography at the end of this catalogue includes many more books than are actually cited in Klooster's text and does not include a few items that at the last minute we decided to put on display at the Equitable Gallery. We intend to prepare at a later date a simple list of all of the pieces on exhibition, including even the ten or fifteen items not from the John Carter Brown Library. The principal function of the Chronological Bibliography, then, is to offer prospective researchers a sampling, perhaps ten percent, of the Library's treasures on this subject.

As is well known, the longest-standing, uninterrupted treaty of amity and commerce that the United States has with any nation is that with the Netherlands, the 200th anniversary of which was celebrated in 1982. The exhibition at the Equitable Gallery and this associated publication is one more link in the long chain of mutual appreciation between the two countries.

NORMAN FIERING
The Beatrice and Julio Mario Santo Domingo
Director and Librarian
The John Carter Brown Library

Introduction

This is a tale seldom told. It is the story of a country small in size but with great ambitions that has left its imprint on the Americas since the late sixteenth century. A conglomerate of regions subservient to the Habsburgs, the Netherlands for a long time were little more than a geographical abstraction. After Protestantism had taken root, a rebellion broke out that lasted for eighty years and resulted in the independence of the northern Netherlands. The Dutch Republic rapidly developed into one of the world's major trading nations, sending scores of vessels to Asia, Africa, and the Americas. Trading posts were established in various parts of the New World, but it was Asia that cast a spell on the Dutch merchants. Even the first large-scale westward ventures across the Atlantic were all intended to explore alternative sea-routes to the Far East.

The Dutch East India Company, the largest commercial company the world had ever seen, was soon joined on the global stage by a counterpart for the Western Hemisphere. Initially, however, commerce was not the main priority of the West India Company, even though it was granted a monopoly of trade and shipping to Africa south of the Tropic of Cancer, and to the Americas. In actual practice it was more of a maritime war machine, fighting both Habsburg Spain and Portugal. The Dutch seized hundreds of enemy ships plying between Europe and Latin America and even managed to capture a rich silver fleet, on its way from Mexico to Spain.

Besides, warfare was used as an instrument to promote Dutch colonization. Battles were waged over the Caribbean islands of Curaçao and St. Martin, and Dutch armies entered upon a protracted struggle to conquer and then defend parts of the Portuguese colony of Brazil. Its northeastern captaincy of Pernambuco became the focal point of Dutch interest in all of the Americas. For a quarter of a century, they controlled this important sugar-producing area, but could not hold on to it. A rebellion of Portuguese settlers never lost momentum and, with support from Lisbon, eventually buried Dutch aspirations to greatness in South America.

America lured not only people looking for material gains or those who simply wanted to start anew in another environment. It also attracted Dutch cartographers, biologists, and other scientists who came to amass knowledge of the New World. They set up an astronomical observatory in Dutch Brazil, compiled a vocabulary of an indigenous Chilean language, and discovered numerous butterfly species in Suriname.

Shortly after the Dutch lost Brazil, they were deprived of their North American colony as well.

In 1664, an English squadron conquered New Netherland, the vast area between the Connecticut and Delaware Rivers, just when emigration from the Netherlands finally seemed to be taking off. Although Nieuw Amsterdam was renamed New York, the city did not lose its Dutch character for a good length of time. Political dependence on the Dutch Republic lapsed, but in religion the subordination of the Dutch Reformed Church in America to the Netherlands was not ended until shortly before U.S. independence.

At the Peace of Breda (1667), the loss of New Netherland was offset by the simultaneous acquisition of Suriname, an English settlement recently conquered by a Dutch expedition. At the time, this exchange of New York for Suriname looked like a good bargain. Suriname was a promising agricultural colony, whereas North America had never earned much for the Dutch. In due course, Suriname did become the Dutch plantation colony par excellence, but even then it could never stand comparison with the leading English and French cash crop colonies, such as Barbados and Saint-Domingue.

As they organized tropical agriculture, the Dutch changed the ethnic make-up of their colonies of Suriname, Berbice, Demerara, and Essequibo for good. Hundreds of thousands of slaves were imported from Africa to supply labor for the sugar, cacao, cotton, and tobacco plantations. The islands of Curaçao and St. Eustatius, on the other hand, were hardly termini of the Dutch slave trade, but rather transit stations between Africa and Spanish America. Both Caribbean colonies became major regional entrepôts, where a great variety of goods could be bought and sold.

Thus in their own ways, explorers, scientists, scholars, traders, and settlers from the Netherlands have helped shape the New World from the Hudson River to the Strait of Magellan. On the face of it, little is left of their exploits. When Trinidadian writer V.S. Naipaul visited British Guiana in the early 1960s, the only artifacts reminiscent of the bygone days of Dutch plantation agriculture along the Essequibo River were "heaps of bricks here and there." On Tobago and in other parts of the Caribbean that once accommodated settlers from the Netherlands, only seasoned archaeologists may be able to find the vestiges of Dutch culture. In another sense, however, there are physical remains. Dutch activities were reflected in contemporary books, many of which are kept at the John Carter Brown Library. Unfortunately, they have remained hidden treasures. The Dutch language is such an obstacle that American historians have rarely opened these books. That is no reason to be ashamed, however, for even their Dutch colleagues are unfamiliar with them. I only immersed myself in this vast body of literature after I first came to the Library in September 1995 as a Fulbright fellow.

Preparing the exhibition would have been impossible without the help of the Library staff. I would like to extend a special word of thanks to Susan Danforth and Burton Van Name Edwards. The text of this catalogue has benefited from fruitful conversations with numerous Library fellows and visitors, and especially from the comments of three experts. I am grateful to professors Patricia Bonomi, Pieter Emmer, and James Tanis for sharing their knowledge and for preventing the perpetuation in print of some vaguenesses, inaccuracies, and errors. My greatest debt, however, goes to the director of the John Carter Brown Library, Dr. Norman Fiering. His encouragement and his passion to make the exhibition a success have meant a lot to me.

Although it interrupted my work on two books, writing this catalogue has been a valuable experience. I can only hope that reading the story of the Dutch in the Americas will be as rewarding an enterprise.

WIM KLOOSTER

Chronology

1477 Marriage of Mary of Burgundy to Archduke Maximilian of Habsburg

1566 Radical Calvinist iconoclastic fury sweeps the Netherlands

1568 Start of the Eighty Years War

1579 Founding of the Union of Utrecht

1584 Assassination of William of Orange

1596 Publication of Van Linschoten's *Itinerario*

1596 Dutch build fort at Essequibo

1596-97 Discovery of Spitsbergen by Willem Barentsz

1598 Expedition of Mahu and De Cordes to the Strait of Magellan

1598-99 Expedition to establish commercial relations with the Río de la Plata

1599 Failed retaliation mission of Dutch against Spain in the Atlantic

1602 Founding of the VOC, the Dutch East India Company

1607-08 English Pilgrims move to the Netherlands

1609 The *Halve Maen* sails to the Hudson River

1609-21 Twelve Year Truce between Spain and the United Provinces

1615 Voyage of Le Maire and Schouten to southern South America

1618 Coup d'état of Prince Maurits

1621 Founding of the Dutch West India Company

1624 Start of colonization of New Netherland

1624-25 Dutch occupation of Bahia in Brazil

1627 Berbice in Guiana becomes a patroonship

1628 Zeeland settlement founded on Tobago

1628 Piet Heyn's capture of the New Spain Silver Fleet

1630 Capture of Recife in Brazil

1637-44 Governorship of Johan Maurits in New Holland

1637 Conquest of São Jorge da Mina on the West African Gold Coast

1643 Dutch conflict with New Netherland Indians

1643 Expedition to conquer Chile

1645 Start of Brazilian rebellion against Dutch

1647-64 Governorship of Pieter Stuyvesant in New Netherland

1648 Battle of the Guararapes in Brazil leaves 957 Dutchmen dead

1648 Peace Treaty of Munster between Spain and the United Provinces

1654 Capitulation of Dutch in Brazil

1655 Dutch conquest of New Sweden on the Delaware

1663 French conquest of Dutch Cayenne

1664 English conquest of New Netherland

1667 Successful Zeeland invasion of Suriname

1673 Failed French invasion of Curaçao

1673-74 Brief Dutch reconquest of New Netherland

1678 French conquest of Tobago

1685 Synagogue erected in the Jewish Savannah in Suriname

1689 Leisler's rebellion in New York City

1732 New synagogue finished in Curaçao

1763-64 Large-scale slave rebellion in Berbice

1772 End to subordination of Dutch Reformed Church in America to the Reformed Church of the Netherlands

1776 Salute to *Andrew Doria* at St. Eustatius tantamount to Dutch recognition of the United States

1781 British assault on St. Eustatius

1782 Dutch recognize John Adams as official envoy of the United States

1795 French invasion ends the Dutch Republic

1796 British invasion of Demerara, Essequibo, and Berbice

The Dutch in the Americas

FIG. 1.1 Willem Schouten, the first man to round Cape Horn. In this pantheon, he is put on a level with Magellan, while Cavendish, Drake, and two Dutchmen, Joris Spilbergen and Olivier van Noort, are also present. From Willem Cornelisz. Schouten, *Iournael ofte beschryving vande wonderlijcke voyagie* (Dokkum, 1649).

CHAPTER 1

The Birth of the Dutch Republic and the World War Against Habsburg Spain

States hardly ever begin their lives as world powers, but in the seventeenth century a federal republic emerged from an eighty years war possessing more ships than the rest of Europe combined, in command of a vast colonial empire, and engaged in trade in all quarters of the globe. It was the heyday of the United Provinces, what might be called the Dutch Republic's Golden Age. In the opinion of the great Dutch historian Johan Huizinga, however, the latter term was inappropriate. "Golden Age" smacked of the mythical land of Cockaigne, Huizinga said. If our florescence has to be named, he argued, let it be for wood and steel, pitch and tar, paint and ink, guts and godliness, spirit and fantasy.

The Rise of the Northern Netherlands

Commercial development and industrial output in the northern Netherlands were impressive. Before the middle of the seventeenth century, the Dutch carrying trade was unrivalled internationally. Wood and steel, pitch and tar underwrote thriving arts and sciences; spirit and fantasy found expression in the development and application of imported inventions, such as fortress-building and cartography. But there was also an original side to the Dutch artistic boom. Painting, for instance, flowered in a style of its own that had been developed since its gradual departure from Mediterranean models in the fifteenth century.

It may not be obvious, at first sight, why the northern Netherlands were able to become the pivotal commercial center in Europe. Economic, political, as well as religious factors account for this extraordinary development. In the late Middle Ages, the trade and industry of the northern Netherlands had lagged far behind the southern provinces. The urban-based textile industry of the southern Netherlands dominated many foreign markets, with first Bruges and later Antwerp growing into centers of commerce that attracted merchants from all over Western Europe. But meanwhile, the coastal province of Holland was developing into the economic center of the North. A transition had occurred from agrarian farming to stock-breeding, while diking and poldering, going on for centuries, made possible the vast reclamation of fens. The colonization of new lands resulted in the emergence of an independent peasantry, free from feudal obligations and free to settle wherever they liked. Many people freed from the land began to earn a living in shipping and trade, particularly the grain trade, which became an Amsterdam specialty. Supplies of grain from France and England were soon overshadowed by grain transported from the Baltic, which not only served to feed the Dutch, but was trans-shipped increasingly also to southern Europe.

Despite this economic progress, politically the provinces comprising the Low Countries were lacking in unity. Disjunctions within the Holy Roman Empire cleared the way for strong regional entities, such as the duchy of Brabant and the counties of Flanders, Holland, Zeeland, and Hainault. In the course of the fifteenth century, these areas were acquired by the Burgundian dynasty. In this period as well, the new rulers introduced the States General, a lasting federal-type institution initially made up of provincial representatives of the clergy, the nobility, and the commons.

Mary of Burgundy's marriage in 1477 to Archduke Maximilian of Habsburg was a turning-point in Dutch history. Maximilian's son Philip would one day be the paramount ruler of the Netherlands, and Philip's son Charles V was to inherit the Burgundian territories there. When Charles succeeded to the crowns of Castile and Aragon, he established his chief residence in Spain, leaving the day-to-day government of the Netherlands in the years ahead to appointed governors. Their pursuit of centralization encountered stiff resistance, and various revolts had to be put down before the unification of the seventeen provinces was accomplished. The annexation of the eastern duchy of Gelderland in 1543 completed the process of political integration of the Low Countries, consisting of present-day Belgium, the Netherlands, and Luxemburg. This achievement, however, was to be short-lived.

In these countries, Protestantism found receptive ground. Reformers directed their criticism against a number of perceived Church abuses including hagiolatry, ecclesiastical taxes, and the increase in revenue-producing offices, a phenomenon that was becoming rampant at all church levels. Reformist activities were scattered, unorganized, and diverse. Indigenous movements rooted in the fifteenth and early sixteenth centuries grew side-by-side with imported Lutheran gatherings. Radical groups, such as the Anabaptists, eschewing infant baptism and questioning many of the other teachings of traditional Christianity, were also spreading by the 1520s. By the 1550s, however, Calvinism was moving from France into the southern Netherlands and was gradually spreading from there into the northern provinces. In addition to purely theological differences, Calvinism varied significantly from Lutheranism in its stance on church-state issues. Calvin envisaged a much greater role for the church in affairs of state.

In Flanders, where Calvinism had made many converts, the Reformation suddenly radicalized in 1566. People from all walks of life, some of them hungry, others variously dissatisfied, and all affected by a grave economic crisis, vented their anger on the Catholic Church in an unparalleled iconoclastic fury. The rebellion traveled like a heathland fire from western Flanders to Groningen in the northeast of the Netherlands. Within the path of destruction, the interiors of scores of Roman Catholic churches were smashed to pieces, and the images of saints in particular demolished.

Resolved to stamp out heresy, the Spanish king Philip II sent an army under the Duke of Alba to bring the rebellious provinces to heel. Alba was commissioned to take strong measures. He set up a Council with the authority to indict and judge all participants in the recent events. Over twelve thousand Netherlanders of every station in life were victims of this "Council of Blood," as it was known to its enemies. Other measures introduced by Alba included the imposition of permanent taxes on the sale of personal property and real estate, a move that antagonized merchants and provincial bureaucrats alike and drove many into the arms of the rebels.

The besieged Dutch were fortunate that a strong leader emerged, William of Orange (1533-1584), count of Nassau in Germany, and prince of Orange, a wealthy principality in southern France. His military and administrative career in the service of Charles V had earned Orange a seat in the Council of State, the principal advisory group of the governor of the Netherlands. For a long time, this Council was the pillar of Spanish Habsburg authority, until Philip II embarked on his autocratic policy. The noble Council members, however, were too much linked to the provinces to leave the Spanish king to his own devices.

Orange, who was known as "William the Silent," served as the commander-in-chief of the anti-Spanish forces in his capacity of stadholder, i.e., a chief provincial officer. This responsibility put him in the position, paradoxically, of both representing the provinces of Holland, Zeeland, and Utrecht, where he was a stadholder, and at the same time exercising military authority over them. Four years after he had first engaged his mercenary army in battle, without much success in the offense, Orange heard the good news that the Zeeland town of Brill had fallen into patriot hands. This martial exploit of 1572 by the so-called Sea-Beggars, a group of exiled Dutchmen who had taken up privateering, was a foretaste of better times. With the initiative moving

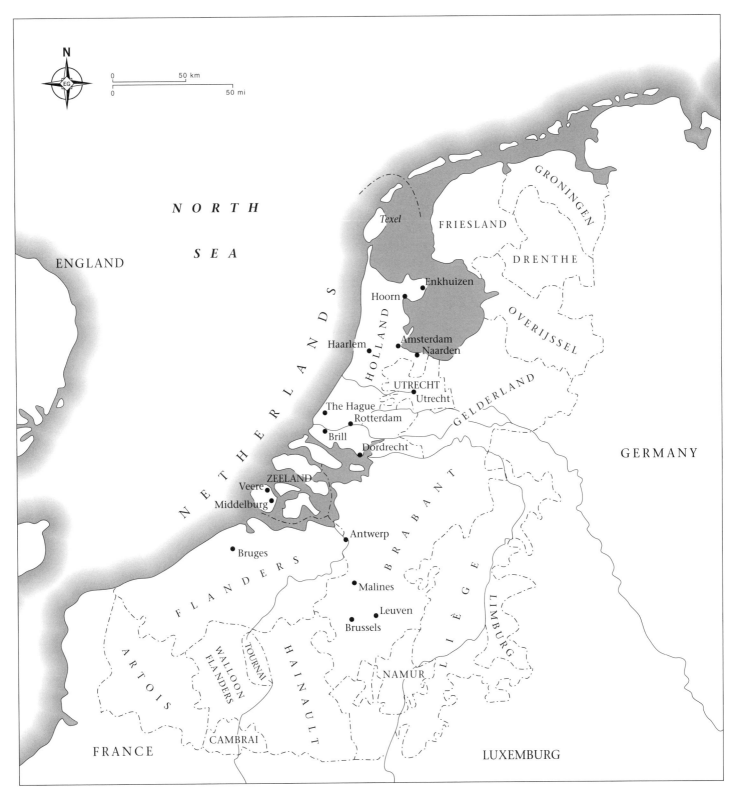

NORTH

SEA

ENGLAND

Texel

FRIESLAND

GRONINGEN

DRENTHE

N E T H E R L A N D S

HOLLAND

OVERIJSSEL

Enkhuizen

Hoorn

Haarlem

Amsterdam
Naarden

UTRECHT
Utrecht

GELDERLAND

The Hague

Rotterdam

Brill

Dordrecht

GERMANY

ZEELAND

Veere

Middelburg

BRABANT

Antwerp

Bruges

Malines

LIÈGE

Leuven

LIMBURG

Brussels

FLANDERS

ARTOIS

WALLOON
FLANDERS

TOURNAI

HAINAULT

NAMUR

CAMBRAI

FRANCE

LUXEMBURG

MAP I The Netherlands, ca. 1600

to the Protestants and their allies, concerted action was imperative. Orange's "own" provinces joined together with towns in Friesland, Flanders, and Brabant, as well as with the rural parts of Groningen, in forming the Union of Utrecht in 1579. This political agreement, promising financial and military cooperation, became the founding constitution of the United Provinces of the Netherlands. It was there and then that the seeds of the Dutch Republic were planted.

A major setback for the northern provinces occurred in 1584, when a French assassin, lured by a reward Philip II had offered, shot and killed William the Silent. Fortunately, William left a very competent son, prince Maurits (1567-1625), who was appointed a stadholder and the captain-general of the Union. Under his command, essential military reforms were carried out. The tightening of discipline was at the heart of the reforms, which included improved training and drill, as well as the standardization of weaponry and ammunition. The number of musketeers in relation to pikemen was increased, and the army was reorganized into smaller formations. Funded by profits from trade and shipping, these military innovations underlay the impressive performance by the Dutch in their war against Spain's formidable army of Flanders.

The Fight for Independence Becomes a Global War

In the 1590s, Dutch trade was expanding in all directions, and before long, hundreds of ships were sailing to Africa, Asia, and the Americas. This sudden worldwide expansion was not only economically motivated. Another objective was to damage Spain and Portugal. War with the Iberian states, which in 1581 were united under one crown, entered upon a new stage as the Dutch continued their hostilities in the Iberian colonies all over the world. In fact, trade and warfare were inseparable; carrying the war to the colonies was integral to the goals of trade.

The first Dutch successes were achieved in the Far East. Since 1602, Dutch activities in Asia had been coordinated by the East India Company, or the VOC, which was created to end cutthroat competition among the numerous Dutch merchants who had plunged into the spice trade. But there was another reason the States General granted the VOC a charter: the perception that the Company could be an efficient instrument of war against the Iberians [13].[1]

The Company was given extensive powers for this end. Its privileges included the construction of forts in the charter area, and the power to declare war and to conclude treaties with indigenous princes.

Although in later years the VOC would grow into the largest commercial company in the world, its first successes were essentially military. The Portuguese-held Moluccas were conquered and an offensive was started to capture Malacca, where the Portuguese had also established themselves.

In the Atlantic, Dutch achievements were still a faint reflection of Asian exploits. In 1599, an expedition of seventy-three sail got underway with the aim of retaliating against the embargo that King Philip II's son and successor Philip III had imposed on Dutch shipping. The objectives of the mission were to cut Spain off from its American provinces and to occupy some Iberian islands in the Atlantic. Although the plans leaked out, enabling the enemy to prepare, the Canary Islands were attacked and the Portuguese island of São Tomé was conquered. The Admiral of this fleet died from an infectious disease early in this campaign, but, undeterred, a small squadron crossed to Bahia and tried in vain to seize the Brazilian port [21].[2]

Subsequent attempts in this period to seize strategic territories in the Atlantic were also beset by failure: the war fleet of six ships that sailed to Brazil in 1604 to found a fort was no more successful than the army dispatched to seize Portugal's West African forts of São Jorge da Mina and Axim, two years later. On the other hand, a few small Dutch settlements did come into being in Guiana, and Dutch ships had begun explorations in the Strait of Magellan. Back in Europe, the war in the Netherlands reached a standoff in the campaigns of 1606 and 1607, but the Dutch scored a major victory at sea in 1607, destroying a Spanish fleet at Gibraltar in April. The Spaniards watched these developments with growing anxiety, and during the negotiations for an armistice, they made the Dutch presence in Asia as well as the Americas a central issue. Aside from his concerns about religion in the Low Countries, Philip III was willing to recognize the seven northern provinces of the Netherlands as a sovereign state only on the condition that they halt the progress of the East India Company and abandon plans to create a similar company for the Western Hemisphere. The chief Dutch negotiator, Johan van Oldenbarnevelt, was ready to deliver up this trump-

---

1 *Discours by forme van remonstrantye: vervatende de nootsaecke-lickheydt vande Oost-Indische navigatie* ("Discours in the form of a remonstrance: concerning the need for East Indian navigation"). Netherlands, 1608.

2 Johann von Leubelfing, *Ein schön lustig Reissbuch* ("A merry travel book"). Ulm, 1612.

FIG. 1.2 Two natives of the Río de la Plata, a region visited in 1598-99 by two Dutch ships. From Hendrick Ottsen, *Iournael oft daghelijcx-register* (Amsterdam, 1617).

Inhabitantes fluuij . Rio de la plata

N°4

card for the sake of peace, but he was thwarted by the combined force of Prince Maurits, the powerful long-distance traders, the Calvinist clergy, and numerous military officers. The resulting compromise was the Twelve-Year Truce between the States General of the United Provinces, King Philip III, and their respective leaders in the Northern and Southern Netherlands.

Early Explorations

The destination of the first Dutch voyages to the New World was the Wild Coast, that vast and practically uninhabited littoral between Venezuela and Brazil. The silver mines Sir Walter Raleigh had described had stirred the imagination of some Zeelanders, such as the mayor of Middelburg who fitted out a ship of three hundred tons "to visit the river called Dorado, situated in America." Similar expeditions saw the establishment of trading posts on the Amazon and Essequibo rivers, where "factors," i.e. traders, were left behind with some merchandise. Encounters with nearby Indians at this time were, almost without exception, relatively peaceful, but the harmony did not lead to a lively exchange of goods. Everywhere, Indian demand fell short of Dutch expectations.

From these outposts, it was always possible to venture out on privateering or marauding expeditions against Spain, when the peaceful exchange of goods was unrewarding. Such was the case in the pearl trade off the coast of Nueva Andalucía, present-day Venezuela. Dutch vessels typically would wait in the area for pearl fisher boats to pass and then barter to obtain this precious cargo. But on other occasions, Dutch bottoms simply attacked Spanish ships and stole the cargo. These acts of piracy took on such proportions that pearls temporarily, because of the short supply, could no longer serve as a local currency.

By the beginning of the seventeenth century, the search for pearls had become a luxury for the Dutch. Most Dutch ships sailing to the Caribbean were now looking for something much more bulky and much more essential: salt. The Dutch used salt to make butter and cheese, and in the fishing industry salt was needed for the pickling of meat and the curing of bacon on board ships. It was also an important exchange commodity in the Baltic trade. When Philip III's embargo banned Dutch ships from the salt of Andalusia and Setúbal in Iberia, the Netherlanders turned to a natural salt-lagoon in Punta de Araya, eastern Venezuela.

Araya salt was obtained not through trade, but by the Dutch collecting it themselves. Because of the sweltering temperatures, the mariners wore wooden shoes instead of boots. They broke the hard salt under the surface of the water with iron bars. The labor was so heavy it could only be undertaken in the early morning or late afternoon. Fortunately, Punta de Araya salt was rendered superfluous by the signing of the Truce of 1609, which meant that the Dutch could once again enter Setúbal.

The Dutch presence in the Caribbean continued, however. A regular illicit trade was developing with Santo Domingo, which was so successful that the Spanish authorities, in order to thwart it, ordered the depopulation of the northern coastal area, roughly the area of present-day Haiti. A Dutch fleet of sixteen ships, which was lying in the bay of Gonaives, hastened to help the people who were forcibly evacuated in the name of prince Maurits, but did not get a response. The terms for Dutch assistance were probably too great an obstacle: they included the citizens' abjuration of the king of Spain and the renunciation of their Roman Catholic faith.

Other parts of the Americas attracted Dutch attention as well, although not always with positive results. Two ships in 1598-99 were defeated in their attempt to establish commercial relations with the Río de la Plata, the region of present-day Buenos Aires. The ships' names, the *Golden World* and the *Silver World*, are a good indication of their owners' hopes. They seemed to have good prospects for trade, but when eleven mariners went ashore and attended Mass "to light a candle for the devil," they were clapped in irons. A final endeavor to open trade with Bahia also failed, and the leader of this venture, Hendrick Ottsen, ended up in a Portuguese prison. Ottsen published the story of his voyage in: *Iournael oft daghelijcx-register van de voyagie na Rio de Plata* (Amsterdam, 1617) [**23**].[3]

By the time the Dutch had begun systematic oceanic ventures at the end of the sixteenth century, Spain, Portugal, France, and England had already discovered, described, mapped, and charted large parts of the world. Some individuals from the northern Netherlands, however, had earlier visited remote regions, and some had chosen the New World to try their luck. They were clearly outnumbered in the Americas by settlers from Flanders, among whom they were classed for practical purposes. As a group, however, the commercial ascendancy of these northern Netherlanders was such that in the mid-sixteenth century, one of the streets off the central square of Mexico City was dubbed "the street of the Flemings."

Other Dutchmen were found in Asia. One of them was Dirck Gerritzoon Pomp (1544 or 1545 - ca. 1608) from Enkhuizen, who as a boy of eleven was sent to Lisbon by his parents in order to learn the Portuguese language. Making a career in Portuguese service in Asia, he rose to the rank of constable, and found himself on board a merchantman that trav-

elled as far as Macao and Nagasaki. Another case was Jan Huygen van Linschoten (1563-1611), who had gone to Goa in 1584 as an employee of the German financial company, the House of Fugger, and had come from the same town as Pomp. After having served the archbishop of Goa, Linschoten returned to Enkhuizen in 1592, carrying notes which he worked up and published three years later. The book, entitled *Reys-gheschrift*[4], was often used as a guide in the following years on voyages to distant destinations. In 1596 Linschoten published his superb *Itinerario* [**5**], a magnificent panorama of pictures and maps of the non-European world. *Itinerario* contained so much detailed and accurate information about shipping lanes, winds, and currents, that seafarers could use it virtually as a handbook. Many of his maps were in fact copies of the excellent models of the Portuguese cartographer Fernão Vaz Dourado. Given the author's firsthand experience, the book obviously was most useful as a source of information about Asia, although Linschoten was also interested in the Americas. He showed this by translating José de Acosta's *Historia natural y moral de las Indias* from Spanish into Dutch,[5] a work that found ready buyers in the Netherlands.

While military strategy, curiosity, and the pursuit of profit drove the Dutch to other continents, their voyages were possible only because of the mushrooming growth of the shipbuilding industry and the remarkable development of navigation techniques. A number of solid devices and techniques were now available to determine latitude, and the charts were constantly improving, but finding longitude at sea remained problematic, despite the claims of some Dutch "inventors" who believed they had discovered a convenient means. One of them was Petrus Plancius (1552-1622), a Calvinist minister originally from Flanders. In his adopted fatherland, Plancius, among other enterprises, collaborated on a translation of the Bible. A man of wide interests, he also applied for a patent on a method to determine longitude, and earned himself a reputation as a mapmaker and a manufacturer of globes and navigational instruments.

In general, cartography had made much headway in the Netherlands in the sixteenth century. Progress in the discipline was indebted to Gemma Frisius (1508-1555), a medical doctor from Friesland who

---

3 "Journal or daily register of the voyage to Río de la Plata."
4 "Travel account."
5 *Historie naturael ende morael van de Westersche Indien* (Enkhuizen, 1598).

FIG. 1.3 During one of
their arctic voyages in the
1590s, the Dutch lost a
ship. They built a new one
in the bitter cold. From
Gerrit de Veer, *Vraye
description de trois voyages*
(Amsterdam, 1598).

established a reputation for himself in the university town of Leuven in the southern Netherlands. His pupils included the famous Gerardus Mercator (1512-1594). Born near Antwerp, Mercator became one of the leading cartographers of his time. His pathbreaking contribution to mapmaking was to project the meridians equally spaced in parallel vertical lines, and the latitudes as parallel horizontal lines, spaced further and further apart as their distance from the Equator increased. Mercator was also the first in 1538 to use the names North and South America on a map. Mercator's name was attached to many subsequent atlases that derived from his work, such as the famous world atlas *Gerardi Mercatoris et I. Hondii. Atlas novus, sive descriptio geographica totius orbis terrarum* (Amsterdam, 1638) [**56**],[6] covering "all lands."

Mercator was accompanied on various journeys by a younger friend, Abraham Ortelius (1527-1598) from Antwerp, whom Mercator urged to publish his *Theatrum orbis terrarum* (Antwerp, 1570) [**2**],[7] an exemplary atlas containing over fifty maps, based on the work of the best geographers, including a map of the New World. Ortelius's atlas was translated into six languages and inspired Lucas Jansz. Waghenaer (1533 or 1534-1604) from Enkhuizen to print his famous *Spieghel der Zeevaert* ("Mirror of Navigation"), a combination of traditional geographical descriptions and coastal profiles, with modern sea charts

engraved on copper plates. Owing to the clear sailing directions for European coastal waters, Waghenaer's *Spieghel* caught on and was translated into Latin, German, French, and English.

The plates for the *Mariner's Mirrour*, an English version of Waghenaer, were engraved by the Flemish cartographer, engraver, and calligrapher Jodocus Hondius, Sr. (1563-1612). In the early years of the seventeenth century, Hondius was part of what was once called the Flemish school of cartographers, referring to a group of Calvinist families that had settled down in Amsterdam. Intermarriages strengthened the mutual bonds between the Hondius, Kaerius, Montanus, and Janssonius families. They were rivaled in Europe only by the Holland school, about which more will be said below.

The "geo-theologian" Plancius worked independently of the Flemish families. In concert with other restless souls, he organized a number of reconnaissances in the 1590s. They were all intended to find a faster sea route to Asia, especially to the spice islands of Indonesia. Plancius was among those convinced that there existed a seaway to the north of Russia, and posited that an ice-free passage could be found

6 "Gerardus Mercator's and I. Hondius's New atlas, or a geographical description of all lands in the world."
7 "Theatre of the countries of the world."

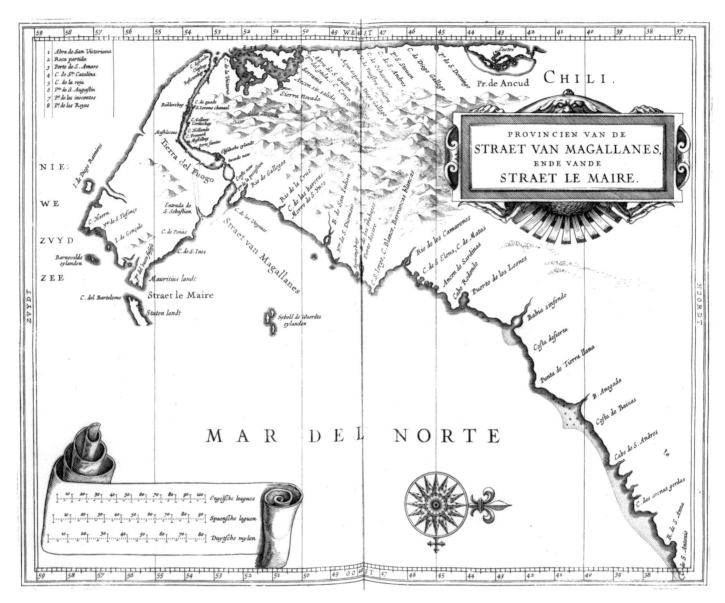

FIG. 1.4 Several Dutch expeditions explored the Strait of Magellan in the late sixteenth
and early seventeenth centuries. From Joannes de Laet, *Nieuvve wereldt* (Leiden, 1625).

FIG. 1.5 The fleet led by Mahu and De Cordes soon ran out of food supplies in the Strait of Magellan. Although many penguins were killed to replenish food stocks, at least one hundred men died. From Barent Iansz. Potgieter, *VVijdtloopigh verhael* (Amsterdam, 1600).

to the east of Novaya Zemlya. The vicissitudes of three such arctic voyages were described by Gerrit de Veer, in two of which the author himself had taken part [**7**].[8] On the remarkable third voyage of 1596-97, Willem Barentsz failed to find a northeast passage, but discovered Spitsbergen. When large amounts of ice east of Novaya Zemlya blocked further progress, Barentsz and his men survived by building a house of driftwood, spending some months north of the arctic circle. Barentsz died five days after the Dutch had finally escaped from their arctic dwelling.

The search for a northeast passage was thereafter mostly given up, but one of its by-products was the realization by the Dutch that there were large numbers of whales in northern waters. Arctic whaling soon developed into a significant activity, despite its incredible hardships. In 1614, a number of Dutch whaling companies united in the Noordse Compagnie, which was granted a three-year fishing monopoly off Novaya Zemlya, Spitsbergen, and Greenland [**100**].[9] By the 1680s, Dutch ships were taking 1,000 whales a year. The classic book on the Dutch whale fishery near Greenland since the time of the first explorations appeared in 1720: *C:G: Zorgdragers bloeyende opkomst der aloude en hedendaagsche Groenlandsche visschery* (Amsterdam) [**133**].[10]

The Strait of Magellan

Enthusiasm about new trading opportunities knew no bounds after the return of a few ships from the fleet of Cornelis de Houtman, which had embarked on a trading voyage via the Cape of Good Hope to Asia in 1597. In the Spring of the following year, three more fleets were fitted out to head for the East Indies by following the same course. But at the same time, a western route through the Strait of Magellan was also tried. Only Magellan himself, Francis Drake, and Thomas Cavendish had preceded the Dutch through the Strait when five ships left the port of Rotterdam in the summer of 1598 and set sail, via the Cape Verde Islands and West Africa, for the extreme south of South America. The venture was led by General Jacques Mahu (1564-1598) and Vice-Admiral Simon de Cordes (ca. 1559-1599).

The voyage seemed ill-starred from the outset. The sick-berth expanded rapidly, there was an acute shortage of water, and in the Strait the mariners were starved into eating raw mussels and penguins. Exhausted from protracted hardships, one hundred out of five hundred men died. Mahu was not spared, nor was Cordes, who was killed by Indians on the island of La Mocha off Chile. Yet in August of 1599,

---

8 *Vraye description de trois voyages*. Amsterdam, 1598. It was translated as: "The true and perfect description of three voyages." London, 1609 [**19**].

9 Jacob Segersz van der Brugge, *Journael, of dagh-register, gehouden by seven matroosen in haer overwinteren op Spitsbergen in Maurits Bay, gelegen in Groenlandt* ("Journal or daily register, kept by seven sailors during their hibernation at Spitsbergen in Maurits Bay, situated in Greenland"). Amsterdam, 1663.

10 "The flourishing rise of the ancient and contemporary Greenland fishery."

to commemorate their defiance of terrible deprivations, as well as to celebrate the planting of Dutch arms in the South American colonies "from where the King of Spain amasses the wealth he uses to sustain a lengthy war against the Netherlands," the six fleet commanders solemnly founded the "Brotherhood of the Unleashed Lion" on the western shores of the Strait [8].[11] Numerous silhouettes of land masses in southern South America, as well as the first comprehensive maps of the Strait of Magellan, were produced by Jan Outghersz., a master of one of the ships, in *Nieuwe volmaeckte beschryvinghe der vervaerlijcker Straete Magellani* (Amsterdam, ca. 1600)[9].[12] Outghersz's maps would remain state of the art for the knowledge of the Strait for the next two centuries.

One of the captains on the Mahu and Cordes expedition was Sebald de Weert (1567-1603), a sea-dog from Antwerp who would later be killed in Ceylon. Because his ship was unable to complete the passage through the Strait, it turned back to Europe. On the way, De Weert discovered the northwestern part of the Falkland Islands, as was reported in *Journael van 't geene vijf schepen . . . over gekomen is, tot den 21. january 1600. toe* (Amsterdam, 1663) [102].[13] The rest of the Dutch fleet emerged from the Strait of Magellan after nine months at sea and subsequently scattered. A few vessels followed the Chilean coast, hoping to pillage the lands of gold they hoped to find further north, but to no avail. One of these ships was commanded by Dirk Gerritsz Pomp, alias "Dirk China" as he had been nicknamed, who had already traveled in Asia. He was taken captive in Valparaiso and only exchanged for Spanish prisoners of war after many years. Another ship sailed to Tidore, one of the Moluccas, where nearly the entire crew was killed, and yet another ship was temporarily lost in the Pacific. Most persons on board this vessel died of scurvy and exhaustion, but two dozen reached Japan in 1600. There they were entertained royally when it became clear that these strangers were not Portuguese. The encounter marked the beginning of the exclusive and long-standing commercial relationship between Japan and the Netherlands.

Like the first one, subsequent Dutch voyages to the Strait of Magellan were not intended simply to reach the Spice Islands along an alternative route. Harming the enemy and capturing a Spanish silver ship were equally important objectives. Such was the case with the next expedition of two ships and two yachts, commanded by Olivier van Noort, an innkeeper from Rotterdam, which put to sea to plunder the west coast of South America. The same harsh fate as had nearly destroyed the previous expedition also befell Van Noort's fleet. When the Strait was reached after eighteen months, many sailors had already died of scurvy, while others had been ambushed in Patagonia. The survivors of the fracas reported that the enemy were cruel-looking, brown-skinned, long-haired giants, with hideously painted faces. Another indigenous attack, during the Dutch passage of the Strait, combined a volley of arrows with a bombardment of penguins. Meanwhile the voyage had not gone unnoticed in the Hispanic world. The viceroy of Peru, anticipating attack, took effective precautions and forced Van Noort and his men to sail home with nothing to show for their pains [25].[14]

After 1602, private or independent traders, that is, those not in the employ of the VOC, were no longer allowed to pass through the Strait. Rounding the Cape of Good Hope and navigation through the Strait were both included as part of the East India Company's monopoly. Yet it was twelve years before the VOC finally fitted out a privateering fleet with the mission of navigating the Strait and seizing a Spanish silver transport. The commander-in-chief was Joris van Spilbergen, who had won his spurs off Africa's west coast and in the waters off Brazil. Although its original goal was not entirely accomplished, Spilbergen's fleet of five ships was more successful than Van Noort's had been. After wreaking havoc in the Chilean towns of Concepción and Valparaiso, Spilbergen defeated a Spanish fleet of eight galleons, sent by the viceroy of Peru, and pillaged Acapulco. Sailing on via the Philippines and the Moluccas, the Dutch fleet completed its trip around the world [24],[15] [28].[16]

Despite the fact that passage through the Strait of Magellan was a VOC privilege, the southwestern

---

11 Barent Iansz. Potgieter, *VVijdtloopigh verhael van tgene de vijf schepen...wedervaren is tot den 7. september 1599. toe* ("Discussion at length of what has happened to the five ships until September 7, 1599"). Amsterdam, 1600.

12 "New updated description of the dangerous Strait of Magellan."

13 "Journal of what happened to five ships until January 21, 1600."

14 Olivier van Noort, *Beschrijvinge van de voyagie om den geheelen werelt-kloot* ("Description of the voyage around the entire world"). Amsterdam, 1618.

15 Joris van Spilbergen, *t'Historiael journael* ("The historical journal"). Amsterdam, 1617.

16 Joris van Spilbergen, *Oost ende West-Indische spiegel der nieuwe navigatien* ("East- and West-Indian mirror of the new voyages"). Leiden, 1619.

ATLANTIC

OCEAN

Strait of Magellan

Isla Grande De

Tierra Del Fuego

PACIFIC

OCEAN

Strait Le Maire

Staten Island

Cape
Horn

N

0   100 km

0   100 mi

MAP II   Strait of Magellan

FIG. 1.6 Dutch musketeers firing at a native vessel shortly after navigating
the Strait of Magellan in 1616. From Willem Cornelisz. Schouten, *Iournael
ofte beschryving vande wonderlijcke voyagie* (Dokkum, 1649).

FIG. 1.7 Dutch explorers Willem Schouten and Jacques le Maire were entertained royally by the native inhabitants of one of the islands in the Strait of Magellan. From Arnoldus Montanus, *De Nieuwe en onbekende weereld* (Amsterdam, 1671).

route to the East Indies was not totally blocked for independent merchants. A former Company director, Isaac Le Maire, a native of French Flanders, ventured to look for another seaway to the Pacific. Le Maire probably doubted the received wisdom that it was Magellan's Strait that separated South America from a vast Antarctic continent, a Southland or Terra Australis Incognita. This mythical southern land mass had shrunk somewhat in the East after the Portuguese rounded the Cape of Good Hope in 1487, but was still believed to have enormous proportions in the West and appeared on scores of maps. Le Maire interested a group of merchants from Hoorn in the formation of an Australian Company, and in 1615 with the approval of the States General, they fitted out the ship *De Eendracht* and a yacht. Commanded by Isaac's son Jacques and the much more experienced Willem Cornelisz Schouten, a man who had made three earlier voyages to the East Indies, the vessels sailed south past the Strait of Magellan. By rounding Tierra del Fuego in early 1616, Le Maire and Schouten proved that it was not part of the alleged great southern continent. The Dutch were under the impression, however, that the next highlands, named "Staten Land" after the States General, did belong to Terra Australis. Jacques Le Maire christened the new passage "Strait Le Maire" after his father, while a sharp corner of Tierra del Fuego was baptized "Cape Hoorn" (Cape Horn) to honor the town of the initiators.

The long voyage, which had brought so many discoveries, had a disheartening ending. The recently arrived governor-general in Batavia on Java, assuming that Le Maire and Schouten had infringed on the VOC monopoly, confiscated *De Eendracht*, attaching no credence to the so-called new seaway. The yacht had been lost previously.

Various accounts of this voyage exist: *Iournal ofte beschryvinghe van de wonderlicke reyse* (Amsterdam, 1618) [26];[17] *Diarium vel descriptio laboriosissimi itineris* (Amsterdam, 1619) [27];[18] and *Iournael ofte beschryving vande wonderlijcke voyagie* (Dokkum, 1649) [81].[19] The crew sailed home on Spilbergen's ships, which happened to be lying in the roads, but Jacques Le Maire died en route.

While the multitude of these voyages across the Atlantic may seem to be scattered and of little economic consequence, the Dutch told themselves to be patient. Realizing the abundance of New World riches, they kept looking for opportunities to establish trading posts. By 1620, they had only succeeded in backwaters of the enemy Iberian empire, such as the Guianas or Venezuela, and also at New Netherland, where no Iberian flag was ever flown. More ambitious designs, however, lay ahead.

---

17 "Journal or description of the curious voyage."
18 "Journal or description of the very laborious voyage."
19 "Journal or description of the curious voyage."

GEZICHT van het WEST~INDISCH~HUYS, op de Binnen plaats te zien, tot Amfterdam.

VUE de la MAISON de la COMPAGNIE des INDES OCCIDENTALES, à Amfterdam.

FIG. 2.1 A view of the inner court of the West India Company headquarters in Amsterdam. H. Schoute, *Gezicht van het West-Indisch-Huys* (Amsterdam, ca. 1790).

CHAPTER 2

The West India Company

By the early years of the seventeenth century, the Dutch were capable of holding off the Spanish Habsburg troops but could not push through. It was evident to both sides that a stalemate had been reached. With neither side able to gain decisive advantages, war-weariness set in. Dutch public opinion was now divided into two camps: a war party and a peace party. Johan van Oldenbarnevelt (1547-1619), Holland's most senior government official, was the champion of the peace party, while Prince Maurits epitomized the war party, which was sustained by dour Calvinists and those interested in privateering and attacks on the Spanish empire. After lengthy negotiations, Oldenbarnevelt was able to impose his will, and a Twelve-Year Truce with Spain was concluded in 1609. The terms contained one stipulation of the greatest significance: the Spanish king recognized the seven United Provinces of the north as "free lands, states and provinces" to which he had no claim. The Twelve-Year Truce also left the territorial boundaries unaltered, thus establishing permanently the partition between the northern provinces of the Netherlands and the southern that later became Belgium, a partition that had existed at least since the Spanish conquest of Antwerp in 1585. Except for a short period in the nineteenth century, each would go their separate ways in history.

Religion had been one of the root causes of the war, and it was not pushed into the background during the Truce. Protestantism was still a minority faith, claiming only ten percent of the population by 1600. It was not until the middle of the century that more than half of the Dutch had left the Catholic Church and joined the Reform movement, influenced theologically by Calvinism in particular. Throughout this period, the social and political implications of Calvinism were under constant discussion. A theological dispute between two Leiden professors, Jacobus Arminius and Franciscus Gomarus, roused emotions and forced citizens to take sides. The Remonstrants, or Arminians, were the more liberal of the two, arguing that individual initiative is an essential element in the process of salvation, and propagating the ideal of a broad church in which a wide range of Protestant beliefs should have a place. The Remonstrants also upheld the notion that the state has the ultimate authority over ecclesiastical affairs. The more dogmatic Calvinist party, the Counter-Remonstrants led by Gomarus, were flatly opposed to these views. Stressing predestination, they advocated a tightening of the orthodox Calvinist doctrine. Seemingly theological issues became heavily politicized when urban secular magistracies from Holland, headed by Oldenbarnevelt, who stood for a broad church, took the Remonstrant ministers under their protection and thereby antagonized the Counter-Remonstrants.

A civil war seemed imminent until Prince Maurits appointed himself the leader of the Counter-Remonstrants and staged a *coup d'état* in 1618, tipping the political balance in the direction of orthodoxy. In this tense atmosphere, a national synod was held in Dordrecht, at which the Remonstrants suffered defeat. Civil judges then stepped in, also finding the Remonstrant leadership guilty, and severe sentences were meted out. Oldenbarnevelt himself refused to back down and was executed in public.

With these victories behind them, it was only a matter of time before Maurits and the war party again took up arms. With the downfall of Oldenbarnevelt, who had strived for a lasting peace, there was no chance of prolonging the Truce when it expired in 1621. Simultaneously with the resumption of hostilities, a new organization made its appearance, the West India Company. The formation of such an entity, oriented toward the Western Hemisphere, had been under discussion for a quarter of a century, but it was not until this moment that all obstacles to it were finally removed. Ideas about a monopoly company that would command the Americas, as a counterpart of the VOC, had first been proposed by the indefatigable Antwerper Willem Usselinx (1567-1647). As a young man, he had travelled extensively and witnessed the arrival of a silver fleet in Seville. A religious refugee, the Flemish Calvinist Usselinx established himself in Middelburg in 1591, shortly afterwards presenting a project to the States General for the organization of a West India Company. It was the first of numerous similar proposals he was to make in the next fifteen years.

Usselinx had a vision of Dutch colonization of the New World. He anticipated, unrealistically, a massive emigration of Netherlanders and expected them somehow to multiply faster than the Iberians had done in Mexico, Peru, and Brazil. The trading company he had in mind was to govern communities where Dutchmen would earn a living both by trade and agriculture. Usselinx was an early advocate of the view that the true riches of the Americas were not to be found in precious metals alone. Look at Brazil, he wrote, a land without gold or silver mines but whose trade is highly profitable because it produces sugar, cotton, brazilwood, and ginger [**16**].[1] Usselinx expected the Native Americans to live in amity with the Dutch, ready to be converted to Calvinism and willing to learn European methods of agriculture. Although the Spaniards had failed to induce the Indians to trade, the Dutch were much more likely to succeed, he believed, since the prices they asked for their manufactures were far below those of Spanish products. A trading company, Usselinx argued, was the obvious means to generate profitable trade with these far-away regions.

Moreover, Usselinx reasoned, Dutch ventures in the New World would have the added advantage of compelling Spain to divert forces to America and thus have a favorable effect on the war at home. The settlement areas Usselinx had primarily in mind were Chile and the Wild Coast, both poorly defended links in Spain's chain of colonies. As late as the 1620s, he was advising against the colonization of North America. Virginia's climate did not lend itself to yielding valuable products, he believed, while Florida was far too cold a place to live.

Finally, in 1606, after his years of urging, the States of Holland greeted one of Usselinx's numerous proposals with approval. They took great pains over his plan to establish a company for the Western Hemisphere, but the Truce with Spain introduced in 1609 stood in the way. Given the importance of the issues, the States General had agreed to the twelve-year ceasefire only after mature consideration, and despite a vociferous campaign by opponents. In 1608 alone, a host of pamphlets was produced pro and con, including *Consideratien vande vrede in Nederlandt gheconcipieert* [**11**];[2] *Dialogus oft tzamen-sprekinge, gemaect op den vrede-handel* [**12**];[3] *Vanden spinnekop ende t'bieken ofte droom-ghedicht* [**17**].[4] In this period, three pamphlets issued from the pen of Usselinx alone. In the first two, he advocated a truce rather than a peace treaty, on the grounds that peace would trigger Flemish remigration, and thus lead to a loss of Dutch prosperity [**14**],[5] [**15**].[6] All these pamphlets were published together in: *Den Nederlandtschen bye-corf: waer ghy beschreven vint, al het*

---

1 *Vertoogh, hoe nootwendich, nut ende profijtelick het sy voor de Vereenighde Nederlanden te behouden de Vryheyt van te handelen op West-Indien, inden vrede metten Coninck van Spaignen* ("A dissertation, to prove how necessary, vital, and profitable it is for the United Netherlands to preserve the freedom of trade with the West Indies, in the peace with the King of Spain"). 1608.

2 "A draft of considerations regarding the peace in the Netherlands."

3 "Dialogue or conversation, held about the peace negotiations."

4 "The spider and the little bee, or fantasy poem."

5 *Bedenckingen over den staet van de vereenichde Nederlanden* ("Thoughts on the state of the united Netherlands").

6 *Naerder bedenckingen, over de zee-vaerdt, coophandel ende neeringhe* ("Further thoughts, on shipping, trade and business").

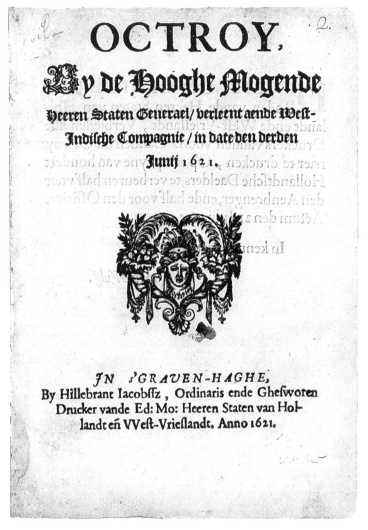

OCTROY,
By de Hooghe Mogende
Heeren Staten Generael/ verleent aende West-
Indische Compagnie / in date den derden
Junij 1621.

IN S'GRAVEN-HAGHE,
By Hillebrant Iacobssz, Ordinaris ende Ghesworen
Drucker vande Ed: Mo: Heeren Staten van Hol-
landt en VVest-Vrieslandt. Anno 1621.

FIG. 2.2 The title-page of the printed charter of the newly-founded West India Company may be translated as follows: "Charter issued by the High Mightinesses the States General to the West India Company on the third of June, 1621." The company was established in part as a war-machine, empowered to maintain an army and a navy, and to conclude treaties.

gene dat nu uytgegaen is op den stilstant ofte vrede [**18**].[7] In any case, the truce with Spain meant that no action on Atlantic ventures could be taken.

As the end of the Truce drew near, however, a growing body of opinion championed the formation at last of a West India Company. Usselinx now found himself only one among many advocates, and the proposal that in the end actually served as a model for the charter of the West India Company was not his. Pushed to the sidelines, Usselinx hoped still to profit from the venture. He audaciously demanded 10 percent of all net revenue that flowed to the state from the West Indies, but despite his early prophetic role as an advocate of Dutch settlement in America, the directors of the new Company had little sympathy for his claims.

The West India Company's charter, issued by the States General on June 3, 1621, was virtually identical to that of the VOC. Both assigned a number of powers and privileges: the right to govern and to administer justice, to conclude treaties with princes, and to maintain an army as well as a fleet [**30**].[8] The WIC was granted a monopoly of trade and shipping to Africa south of the tropic of Cancer, and to the Americas, including the Atlantic islands and the Pacific islands east of New Guinea.

The administrative machinery mirrored the federal polity of the United Provinces, which lacked a strong central government. But although five regional Company boards or chambers were created, in practice just two of them, Amsterdam and Zeeland, controlled the direction of the WIC by virtue of the large share of capital they had invested in it. Amsterdam supplied eight directors and Zeeland four to the Board of the so-called "Nineteen," which was to exercise the highest authority.

One striking difference from the VOC was the interest shown by the common man in westward ventures. Van Noort's expedition had already borne this out, since the financial backers of that voyage included surgeons, goldsmiths, rope-makers, and cloth merchants. Many housewives and maids were now among the subscribers for shares of the West India Company. While the States General granted a one-million-guilder subsidy, the subscription of large money-lenders progressed slowly, despite the use in

---

7 "The Dutch bee-hive: In which you will find all that has so far been published on the Truce or Peace."

8 *Octroy, by de hooghe mogende heeren Staten Generael, verleent aende West-Indische Compagnie in dato den derden Junij 1621* ("Patent, issued by the High Mightinesses the States General to the West India Company on the third of June, 1621"). The Hague, 1621.

several towns of placards with exhortations. One pamphlet, by Usselinx, explained the advantages of subscription: *Korte onderrichtinghe ende vermaeninge aen alle liefhebbers des vaderlandts, om liberalijcken te teeckenen in de West-Indische Compagnie* (Leiden, 1622) [**32**].[9]

It took so long for the WIC to become fully funded that in 1623 the VOC fitted out a venture of its own to the West. The initial hope was that this might be a joint voyage between the two companies, following a design that had become more or less established: passage through the Strait of Magellan, then privateering on the Pacific coast of South America, and finally a Pacific crossing to Asia. The vessels put to sea in April 1623 under the command of Jacques l'Hermite, who would not survive this voyage around the world [**39**].[10] The "Nassau fleet," as it was christened, aimed at intercepting a Spanish silver convoy off the Peruvian port of Arica, but head winds prevented Dutch success. The frustration of this severe setback was worked off on thirty ships lying in Callao and on the port of Guayaquil, which was set on fire. The next scheme also miscarried, when the fleet failed to capture the Manila galleons in Acapulco.

Schemes and Successes

Meanwhile the WIC was at last ready for take-off. The Company was a war instrument first and foremost, which was evident by its emphasis on privateering. Initially, no mention at all was made of colonization and evangelization, objectives that had been central to Usselinx's schemes. He had required even that all colonists be members of the Dutch Reformed Church. He had further anticipated that they would act as missionaries to the natives, proposing the appointment of a council of clergymen and theologians that would coordinate missionary activities.

Despite these concerns, in actual practice warfare prevailed. Among the scenarios discussed initially was an assault on the fort that the Spaniards had built in Araya to keep out the Dutch salt collectors. But preference was given to an attack on the Portuguese colony of Brazil, which had been a destination of Dutch merchantmen since the 1580s. Most of the trade with Brazil was not conducted directly from Dutch ports, but was organized through those of Portugal. Merchantmen left Amsterdam for Lisbon, Viana, or Oporto, sailed to Brazil, and called at Portugal again before returning to Amsterdam. Dutch vessels continued to operate in this circuitous trade even after the implementation of Spanish embargoes, intended to exclude Dutch ships from the Iberian peninsula, and despite the union of the crowns of Spain and Portugal between 1581 and

1640. The continuation of the Brazil trade was made possible by the contacts and efforts of Portuguese "New Christian" merchants (that is, converted Jews), who increasingly took up residence in Amsterdam. Such was the flow of Brazilian sugar that within the city limits of Amsterdam a large number of sugar refineries were established.

Not content with the proceeds of this trade, the Dutch turned their thoughts to the conquest of Brazil, which would give them full control of the sugar economy. Once this plan was born, it was implemented with vigor. The WIC spared no trouble or expense in its attempt to capture Brazil's capital city of Bahia, or Salvador. While 1,637 men had been on board the Nassau fleet in 1623, the Brazil invasion of 1624 numbered twice as many: 3,300. The size of the Dutch fleet which arrived in Bahia frightened off most of the citizens, who fled in panic rather than attempt a military defense. Only the colony's governor and a small number of citizens stayed behind. Shocked by the rapid capture, the Spanish king raised an army of 12,500 men, the largest that had ever crossed the Atlantic, and launched a counter-attack. Waiting in vain for reinforcements, the Dutch garrison was compelled to yield to the superior numbers of the Iberians, after having occupied Bahia for less than a year.

This brief episode led to a host of publications, such as *Reys-boeck van het rijcke Brasilien, Rio de la Plata en de Magallanes* (Dordrecht, 1624) [**33**],[11] which stirred the imagination of the Dutch public. From the Portuguese side, the preparations and reconquest were described by João de Medeiros Corrêa [**35**];[12] and by Bartolomeu Guerreiro [**36**].[13]

Only after the town had already fallen did a Dutch relief force under Boudewijn Hendricksz put in. Realizing it was too late to help in Brazil, Hendricksz sailed to an easier target: Puerto Rico in

---

9 "Short instruction and admonition to all the lovers of the Fatherland, to subscribe liberally to the West India Company."

10 *Iournael vande Nassausche vloot, ofte beschryvingh vande voyagie om den gantschen aerdt-kloot* ("Journal of the Nassau fleet, or description of the voyage around the entire globe"). Amsterdam, 1626.

11 "Travel book of the rich country of Brazil, Río de la Plata, and Magellan."

12 *Relaçam verdadeira de tudo o succedido na restauração da Bahia de Todos os Sanctos* ("True account of all that took place in the restoration of All Saints Bay"). Lisbon, 1625.

13 *Iornada dos vassalos da coroa de Portugal, pera se recuperar a Cidade do Salvador, na Bahya de todos os Santos* ("The day's march of the vassals of the crown of Portugal, to regain the city of Salvador, in All Saints Bay"). Lisbon, 1625.

FIG. 2.3 Panorama featuring the economic productivity of Pernambuco at the time of the Dutch capture of Bahia in 1624, from *Reys-boeck van het rijcke Brasilien* (Dordrecht, 1624).

the Caribbean, arriving there on September 25, 1625. The Spanish governor of that island judged that withdrawal from his headquarters in San Juan would be the prudent step, and left the place to the enemy. The Dutch looted the town and went on a rampage in the Cathedral, but were not able to break the stiff resistance of the Spanish forces which were hiding out in a fort. After a long siege, the Dutch finally gave up. Some of the spoils of this raid, however, came in handy, such as nine church bells that were hung later that year in the building that served as the church tower in Dutch New Amsterdam (later New York).

In the following years, WIC activities were mainly confined to privateering. The Company maintained over a hundred ships and an impressive number of employees, which, including seamen, increased in the decade after 1633 from between 6,000 or 8,000 to 10,000. Johannes de Laet, the Company's contemporary chronicler, claimed that between 1621 and 1637 WIC ships seized over six hundred Iberian vessels, and he estimated the damage they inflicted

at 118 million guilders [**66**]. They netted their best haul in 1628, when the hope of capturing a Spanish treasure fleet was finally realized. For years, plans had been made to strike this blow to the Spaniards, because of its massive consequences for both sides: the WIC would earn a fortune, and it would tear a huge hole in the enemy budget.

Under the leadership of the experienced Admiral Piet Heyn (1577-1629) from Delfshaven, a man who had been the vice-admiral in the assault on Bahia, a Dutch fleet with 2,300 sailors and 1,000 soldiers left the Netherlands in May 1628, with the intention of capturing the silver convoy. The operation had been prepared in such secrecy that even the officers were not informed about the purpose of the expedition. Piet Heyn was allowed to open the instructions only after he had reached the Canary Islands. Once it arrived in the Caribbean, the Dutch fleet of thirty-one sail could not escape the notice of Spanish officials. Throughout the region, Spanish troops were on the alert, but when an entirely different Dutch fleet had left the area after a successful chase by

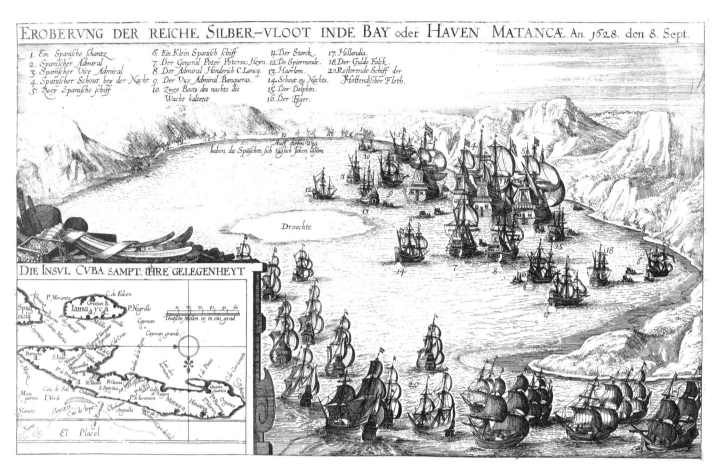

FIG. 2.4 *Eroberung der reiche silber-vloot inde bay oder haven Matancae*
(ca. 1629). In 1628, Dutch warships achieved their greatest success
in the fight against Spanish shipping, subduing a rich Spanish
treasure fleet in the Cuban Bay of Matanzas.

Spanish ships, Spanish authorities believed the way was clear. The Tierra Firme fleet carrying Peruvian silver was held back, but the New Spain fleet, which transported silver from Mexican mines, did put to sea.

Piet Heyn now seized his chance and partly on the open seas east of Havana, partly in the bay of Matanzas, he captured the main part of the New Spain fleet. The total value of the booty, made up of silver, gold, pearls, silk, hides, dyewood, indigo, and cochineal, was 11.5 million guilders, an unbelievable amount of money. While the exuberant Dutch sailors were counting the silver, an activity which lasted for several days, Spanish consternation was immense. The Spanish commander, Juan de Benavides, would die on the scaffold some years afterwards, having been found guilty of negligence. Piet Heyn, on the other hand, was received as a hero by large crowds in The Hague, Leiden, Haarlem, and Amsterdam.

Prior to September 8, 1628, an immortal date in Dutch annals, attitudes in the Netherlands vis-à-vis the Company had been rather sceptical, but the atmosphere suddenly changed after "Matanzas," giving rise to a slew of patriotic writings that kept the memory of Piet Heyn's heroism alive: Salomon Willemssz, *Rapport Gedaen aen hare Ho. Mo.* (The Hague, 1628) [**40**];[14] Rutgerus Eibergen, *Svvymel-klacht des Spaenschen conincks Philippi Quarti, over het eerste verlies van sijn silver-vlote* (Amsterdam, 1629) [**41**];[15] *Practiicke van den Spaanschen aes-sack* (The Hague, 1629) [**43**];[16] Dionysius Spranckhuysen, *Triumphe van vveghen de gheluckighe ende over-rijcke victorie* (Delft, 1629) [**45**].[17] A typical poem ran as follows:

Welcome, welcome, pious hero
With your treasures and your money
Welcome, welcome, noble blood
With your scores of captured goods
Welcome, welcome, welcome, Sir
May such seizures re-occur.[18]

In the meantime, representatives of Spain and the United Provinces were once more gathering around the negotiation table, determined to reach an agreement that would bring about a new truce. Yet others, spurred on by the recent successes in the Western Hemisphere, favored a continuation of the war, as was expressed by a host of pamphleteers. The Spaniards at one point submitted a proposal that was intended to prohibit all Dutch voyages to the East and West Indies. This arrogance infuriated a Dutch pamphleteer: "Most parts of the East and West Indies are unknown to the Kings of Spain, so what right do the Spaniards have to prohibit the Dutch from trading and sailing there? They take pride in the per-

mission of the Pope, but that frivolous allocation of territory is a sheer laughing matter. For he is as much entitled to decide in that matter as the donkey he rides or his most junior kitchen help." [**49**][19]

In the event, no truce was effected and overseas hostilities were allowed to continue. In the year 1630 alone, three Dutch fleets were active in the Caribbean, carrying off prizes and occasionally raiding on shore. But, much as the plundering of ships lying in the Mexican bay of Campeche or the invasion of the town of Trujillo in Honduras may have been efforts worth making in the eyes of the Company shareholders (as explained in *'t Hollandts rommelzootje* [**83**][20]), it was another capture of a treasure fleet that all were waiting for. A serious attempt to bring that about was made in 1638 under the command of one of the most celebrated Dutch admirals, Cornelis Cornelisz. Jol (ca. 1600-1641). According to the plan, "Peg-leg Jol," as he was nicknamed after he had lost a leg at an early age, would make an attack on the Tierra Firme fleet, helped by reinforcements from Europe. But when Jol took the offensive near Cuba, many Dutch captains decided not to take part, and to make matters worse, the promised reinforcements arrived too late. Although subsequent clashes claimed over a hundred Spanish lives, the fleet of seven galleons managed to escape [**58**].[21]

By then, a new age had dawned. Company privateering no longer ran rampant and was replaced by war on land, that developed into the WIC's most ambitious project in the New World: the colonization of Brazil.

---

14 "Report submitted to His High Mightinesses."
15 "Pitiful complaint of the Spanish King Philip IV, on the first loss of his silver fleet."
16 "Practice of the Spanish dustbin."
17 "Triumph upon the happy and very rich victory."
18 *Rym-vieren op de ieghen-woordige victorie, bekomen door den manhaften Generael Pieter Pietersz. Heyn, van Delffs-Haven* ("Rhymed celebration of the present victory, achieved by the brave General Pieter Pieters. Heyn of Delfs-Haven") (The Hague, 1629) [44].
19 *Redenen, waeromme dat de Vereenighde Nederlanden, geensints eenighe vrede met den koningh van Spaignien konnen, mogen, noch behooren te maecken* ("Reasons why the United Netherlands cannot, may not, and should not make any peace with the king of Spain"). The Hague, 1630.
20 *'t Hollandts rommelzootje, vertoonende de gantsche gelegentheyd van het benaaudt, ontzet, en gewapent Amsterdam* ("The Dutch mess, presenting the complete state of anxious, horror-stricken, and armed Amsterdam"). 1650
21 *Translaet uyt den Spaenschen weghens 't gevecht tusschen des conincx silver vloot en d'Admirael Houte-been* ("Translation from the Spanish regarding the fight between the king's silver fleet and Admiral Peg-Leg"). Amsterdam, 1639.

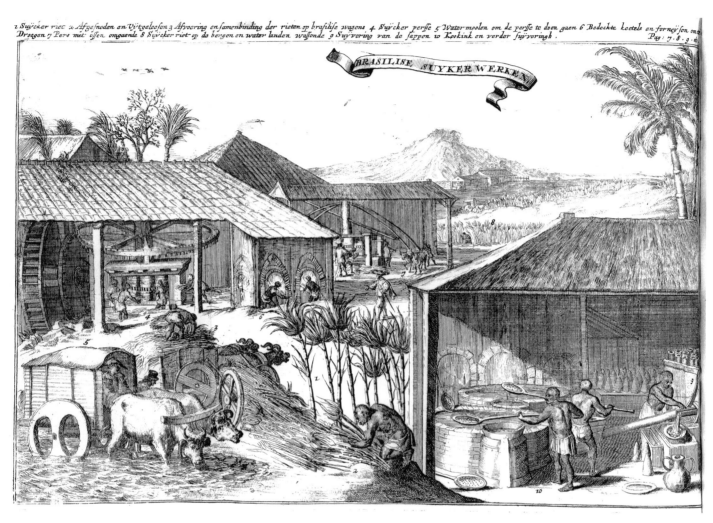

1 Suycker riet 2 Afgesneden en Uytgeleesen 3 Afvoering en samenbinding der rieten op brasilise wagens 4 Suycker persse 5 Water-moolen om de persse te doen gaen 6 Bedeckte keetels en forneysen om
Droogen 7 Pers met ossen omgaende 8 Suycker riet op de bergen en water landen wassende 9 Suyvering van de sappen 10 Kookink en verder suyveringh . Pag: 7. 8. 9 etc

BRASILISE SUYKER WERKEN

FIG. 3.1 The different stages of sugar production in Brazil, from Simon de Vries,
Curieuse aenmerckingen der bysonderste Oost en West-Indische verwonderens-waerdige dingen
(Utrecht, 1682).

CHAPTER 3

The Dutch in Brazil: A Peerless Prince in Pernambuco

Following Piet Heyn's daring exploit in 1628, which greatly enhanced the financial health of the Company, new pleas were made for a military expedition to Brazil. It was soon agreed that 67 ships and over 7,000 men would be sent, under the command of Admiral Hendrik Cornelisz Loncq. In February 1630, the fleet appeared off Recife in the province or captaincy of Pernambuco and conquered the town after a siege of two weeks. Simultaneously, a Dutch landing force overran nearby Olinda, tempting one Dutch artist into lyric imperialist poetry: the naked Mexican, the one-footed cyclops, the envious Chinese, the cruel Patagonian, the black Mozambiquan, and the roguish Sumatran, they all should submit to the immortal Loncq [**46**].[1]

The Beginnings of New Holland

It was clear from the outset that the Spanish king, who at this time represented Portugal as well, intended to fight back vigorously. He sent a powerful fleet to the coast of Brazil, which clashed with a Dutch one dispatched by the States General. In the savage battle that ensued, the Dutch lost five hundred men as well as their flagship, but Spanish and Portuguese losses were even more horrendous. Nevertheless, the Iberians succeeded in landing 700 soldiers, including 300 Neapolitans, to reinforce their land forces. Amplified by Portuguese guerrillas on the scene, which caused no end of trouble, these troops surrounded Recife and left the Dutch in possession of only a small strip of land. Managing to break through the encirclement, the Dutch with the help of Tarairiu Indians embarked on a march of conquest that ended with the occupation of several captaincies from Rio Grande in the north to Cabo de Santo Agostinho in the south. "New Holland," as the colony was called, had suddenly assumed large proportions. Many Portuguese and creoles (i.e., local-born Europeans) now resigned themselves to the new situation, tempted to some degree, no doubt, by Dutch propaganda: the Calvinist promises included freedom of religion as well as tax exemptions.

From the beginning, however, the Dutch paid heavily for their Brazilian adventure. A French observer noted that the health of the Netherlanders was ruined. He saw only weak, skinny men, "not cut out to be soldiers," dying in the hospitals or falling

FIG. 3.2 Title page of a poem in praise of the Dutch conquest of Olinda. From Pieter Baardt, *Friesche Triton* (Leeuwarden, 1630).

---

1 Pieter Baardt, *Petri Baardt Friesche Triton. Over t'geluckich veroveren van de stercke Stadt Olinda, met alle de forten in Fernambucq* ("Pieter Baardt's Frisian Triton. On the successful conquest of the strong town of Olinda, and all forts in Pernambuco"). Leeuwarden, 1630.

FIG. 3.3 The southern part of Pernambuco with the São Francisco River in the top left-hand corner. From Franciscus Plante, *Mauritiados* (Leiden, 1647).

down on the streets, victims of scurvy, dysentery, and worms. Not only were they not immune to certain diseases, the Dutch also lacked experience in waging jungle war. Unlike the enemy, they did not have African slaves at their disposal to carry ammunition and provisions. Back in the United Provinces, reports about massive loss of life tempered optimism. Delegates from Amsterdam and Rotterdam to the States of Holland even advocated the necessity of withdrawal, but they failed to convince other towns.

The "Humanist" Prince

The Polish colonel Krzysztof Arciszewski, who commanded the Dutch troops, constantly argued in favor of an offensive to push the Iberians to the south of the São Francisco River. Only in that way would the Dutch be protected from unexpected guerrilla attacks. His pleas hardly got a response from the quarrelsome leadership of the Dutch colony. The Political Council, the colony's governing body, was always divided, and the authority of the governor, the German Sigismund von Schoppe, was very limited. Accordingly, Arciszewski asked the Nineteen to designate a governor who enjoyed wide powers. Waking up to the necessity of a strongman to rule the colony, the WIC appointed Johan Maurits

FIG. 3.4 Johan Maurits van Nassau-Siegen, the beloved governor of Dutch Brazil, from Caspar van Baerle, *Rerum per octennium in Brasilia* (Amsterdam, 1647). The motto may be loosely translated "Wherever worlds await."

FIG. 3.5 Portrait of Johan Maurits, from Franciscus Plante, *Mauritiados* (Leiden, 1647).

HISTORIA NATVRALIS
BRASILIAE,
Auspicio et Beneficio
ILLVSTRISS. I. MAVRITII COM. NASS. &c.
ILLIVS PROVINCIÆ ET MARIS SVMMI PRÆFECTI ADORNATA
In qua
Non tantum Plantæ et Animalia, sed et In-
digenarum morbi, ingenia et mores describuntur et
Iconibus supra quingentas illustrantur.

LVGDVN. BATAVORVM,
Apud Franciscum Hackium,
et
AMSTELODAMI,
Apud Lud. Elzevirium. 1648.

FIG. 3.6 Title page of Willem Piso, *Historia naturalis Brasiliae* (Leiden and Amsterdam, 1648). The Indians are based on the remarkable ethnographic paintings of Albert Eckhout.

van Nassau-Siegen (1604-1679). This grandson of a younger brother of William of Orange was surely the most remarkable figure to come to Dutch America. He had a versatile mind, an impressive military record, was fluent in several languages—although his tongue reportedly was always twisted when trying to speak Portuguese—and he loved poetry, science, architecture, and painting. Since he was not hesitant to put his predilections into action and was prodigal with money, Johan Maurits left his imprint on the colony, and one might even say, the world.

It is not easy to sum up his achievements in a nutshell. First of all, he persuaded some forty-six scholars, scientists, artists, and craftsmen to leave the comforts of the Netherlands behind them and come over to New Holland to work. This group included Frans Post (1612-1680), a gifted painter of landscapes who came to be called "the Canaletto of Brazil." His engravings were incorporated into Caspar Barlaeus's *Rerum per octennium in Brasilia et alibi nuper gestarum* (Amsterdam, 1647) [71], beautifully edited by Joan Blaeu.[2]

Barlaeus was the pen name of the poet and scholar Caspar van Baerle (1584-1648), who wrote what might be called the official history of Johan Maurits's rule. Besides Frans Post, Albert Eckhout (ca. 1610-1665) and four other painters went to Brazil. Eckhout painted native peoples from life and made a large number of drawings and oil sketches of flora and fauna. His name was long forgotten, until it was rescued from oblivion by Alexander von Humboldt, who saw some of his extraordinary work in the Statens Museum for Kunst in Copenhagen, where the major pieces still remain.

Two outstanding scientists belonged to the governor's entourage: Willem Piso (1611-1678) and Georg Marcgraf (1610-1644). Both were probably encouraged by Johannes de Laet to go to Brazil. Piso came as Johan Maurits's personal physician, but earned a reputation for systematic study of tropical diseases that remained authoritative until well into the nineteenth century. He later became head of medical services in Dutch Brazil. Piso was accompanied by Georg Marcgraf from Saxony, who carried out astronomical observations and put together a survey of Brazil's botany and zoology. Most of the Brazilian plant and animal species mentioned by Marcgraf had not been described before. Johan Maurits sponsored the publication of their findings

---

2 "The events that recently took place in Brazil and elsewhere over an eight-year period."

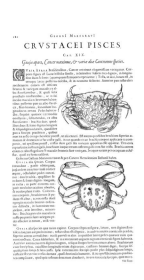

FIGS. 3.7 and 3.8 Willem Piso and his German co-author Georg Marcgraf were among the scholars invited by Governor Johan Maurits to come to Brazil. They published an overview of Brazil's flora and fauna unique for its time. From Willem Piso, *Historia naturalis Brasiliae* (Leiden and Amsterdam, 1648).

in *Historia naturalis Brasiliae* (Leiden and Amsterdam, 1648) [**79**],[3] another magnificent book. Another figure of importance was Zacharias Wagner (1614-1668) from Dresden, a self-taught scholar. Arriving in Brazil as a common soldier, he soon got promoted and served as quartermaster at the court of Johan Maurits. He compiled a *Thier Buch* (Animal Book) containing watercolours of Brazil's wildlife and people. Wagner was later appointed Commander of the Dutch colony at the Cape of Good Hope. Few if any other natural history or ethnographic projects in all of the Americas in the seventeenth century were the equal of these Dutch investigations, taken as a whole.

Johan Maurits had an astronomical observatory built in New Holland, founded a Botanical and Zoological Garden, and even had a new capital built on the island of Antonio Vaz near Recife. Within a few years, Mauritsstad blossomed into a city of six thousand inhabitants, filled with buildings two or three stories high. No trouble or expense was spared either for two estates that sprang up on the same island, Boa Vista and Vrijburg. Spurred on by Johan Maurits's enthusiasm and facilitated by the prospering sugar trade, there was in general impressive building activity in New Holland. The Dutch traveller Johan Nieuhof described in his *Gedenkweerdige Brasiliaense zee-en lant-reize* (Amsterdam, 1682) [**117**][4] how in Recife and Mauritsstad "many burghers were building respectable houses, so that this place is now a fine and elegant town."

The "prince," as the Dutch called him, had an amiable personality and was well-beloved by nearly everyone. Among the Dutch, he succeeded in restoring law and order, which before his arrival had been scarce. His diplomatic skills made him the right man to negotiate with the Indians, and his presence ensured the religious freedom of Jews and Roman Catholics, although Calvinism remained the established religion. Hundreds of Jews immigrated in a few years' time, although—contrary to what is often said—the population of Jews in Dutch Brazil never exceeded that in the Netherlands at the time.

In his protection of Portuguese Catholics, Johan Maurits could not count on the cooperation of most of his fellow Calvinists. It was, perhaps, only to be expected that Dutch ministers spread Protestant propaganda in a Spanish-language tract called "The Reformed Catholic." But the rough Dutch treatment of Portuguese Catholics was quite a different matter.

3 "Natural history of Brazil."
4 "Memorable Brazilian sea and land voyage."

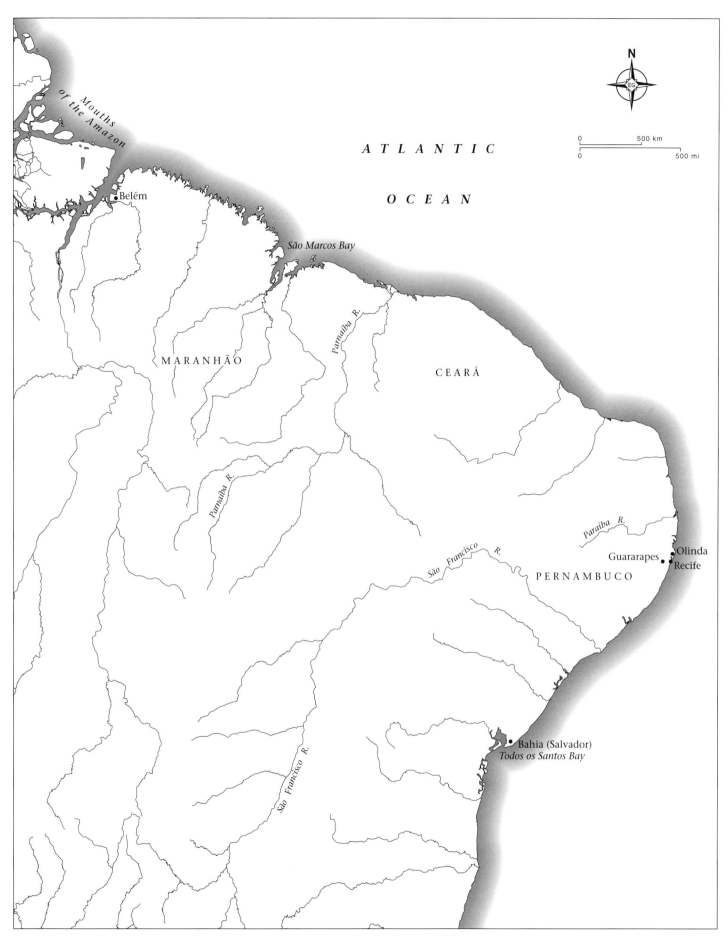

MAP III   Northeastern Brazil

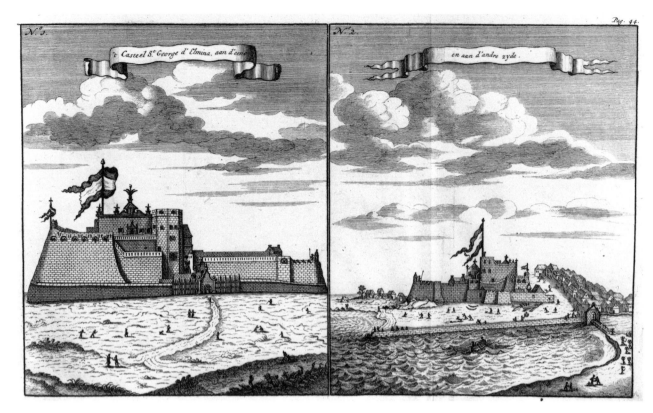

FIG. 3.9 The castle of São Jorge da Mina, wrested by the Dutch from the Portuguese in 1637. "Elmina," as the Dutch called it, became one of the West India Company's slave stations. From Willem Bosman, *Nauwkeurige beschryving van de Guinese Goud-Tand en Slave-kust* (Utrecht, 1704).

A Catholic chapel that Johan Maurits had built for the Portuguese of Olinda, for example, was used instead for Calvinist services. Also, under pressure from the ministers, the Political Council banned saints-day processions and all other external features of the Catholic religion.

Dutch Brazil was made up of two distinct areas: there were the predominantly Calvinist twin cities of Recife and Mauritsstad, and then the settlements in the interior, where Portuguese Catholics were the vast majority and in fact maintained their religion and culture, including processions. The lack of substantial numbers of Dutch settlers was a major weakness of the colony. The West India Company offered inducements for emigration, including free passage, although colonists were expected to pay for their food. Once in Brazil, a piece of land and a dwelling were given to every male settler, the size being proportional to the make-up of his family and the area he intended to till. But despite Johan Maurits's assurance that the fertile soil of Brazil "begs for settlers to inhabit and cultivate this solitude," Dutchmen were little disposed to cross the ocean. Unemployment was not widespread in the United Provinces, and in

those parts of the country where economic conditions were poor, workers were still not so desperate as to contemplate emigration to the vast unknown of America. It is significant that the Dutch outposts in Asia, like the settlements in the Americas, also failed to attract many colonists. A common problem in all the Dutch colonies, regardless of how many came, was that most of those who did migrate were not willing to take up arable farming or plantation agriculture. They rather settled down in the towns and went into trade, or became inn-keepers.

The Beginning of the Dutch Slave Trade

Because the expected immigration of farm hands and maids from the Netherlands failed to materialize, the authorities decided to try the same solution the Portuguese had chosen to meet the labor problem, African slavery, which was universally accepted as a source of labor for the Americas in this era, with hardly any moral stigma. To get access to "human cargoes," a small Dutch force conquered the Portuguese fort of São Jorge da Mina on the West African Gold Coast in 1637, and in 1641-42 Admiral Cornelis Jol launched another successful attack on

PLATE 1. Map of South America from Jan Huygen van Linschoten, *Itinerario* (Amsterdam, 1596). North is to the right.

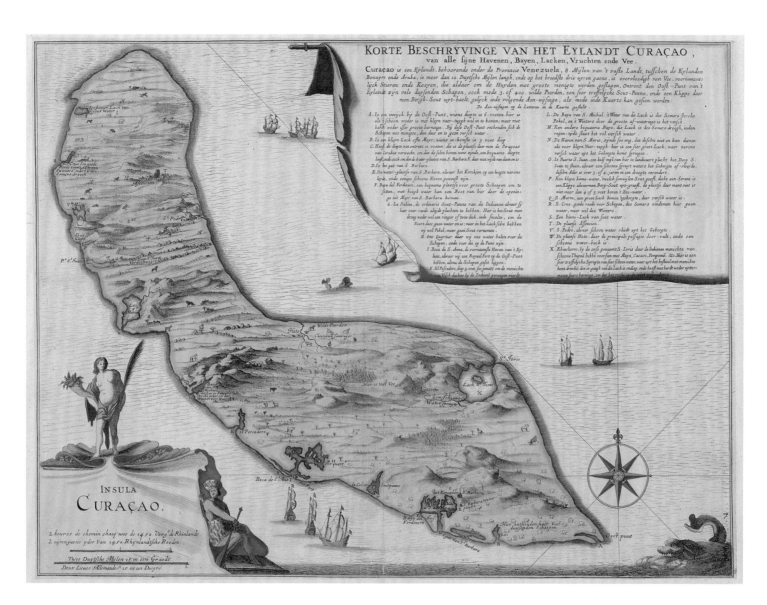

PLATE 2. Map of Curaçao from W. Blaeu, *Tweede deel van 't Tooneel des aerdriicx* (Amsterdam, 1635). Although the accompanying text suggests that Curaçao was still a Spanish colony, a Dutch force had conquered the island one year before the publication of this map.

PLATE 3. Allegorical frontispiece of Joan Blaeu, *Atlas Major*
(Amsterdam, 1662).

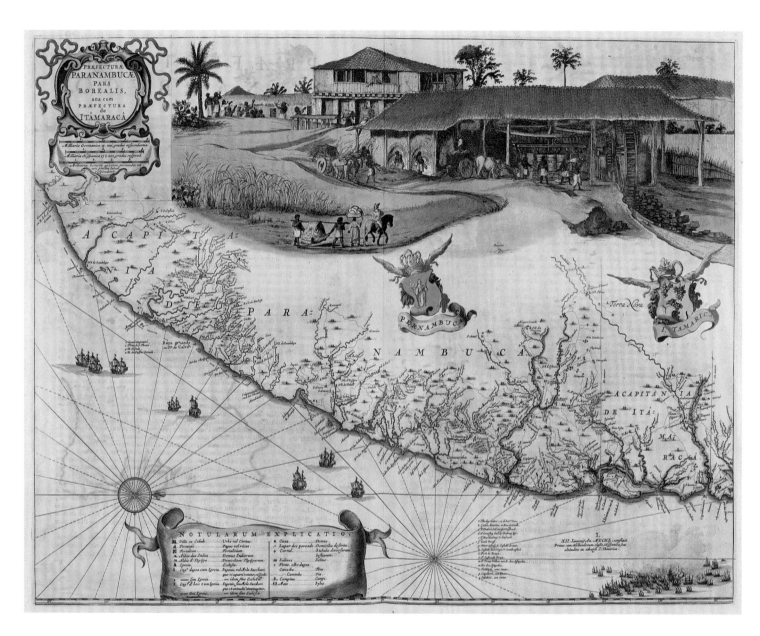

PLATE 4. Sugar plantation in Dutch-held Pernambuco, Brazil. From Joan Blaeu, *Atlas Major* (Amsterdam, 1662).

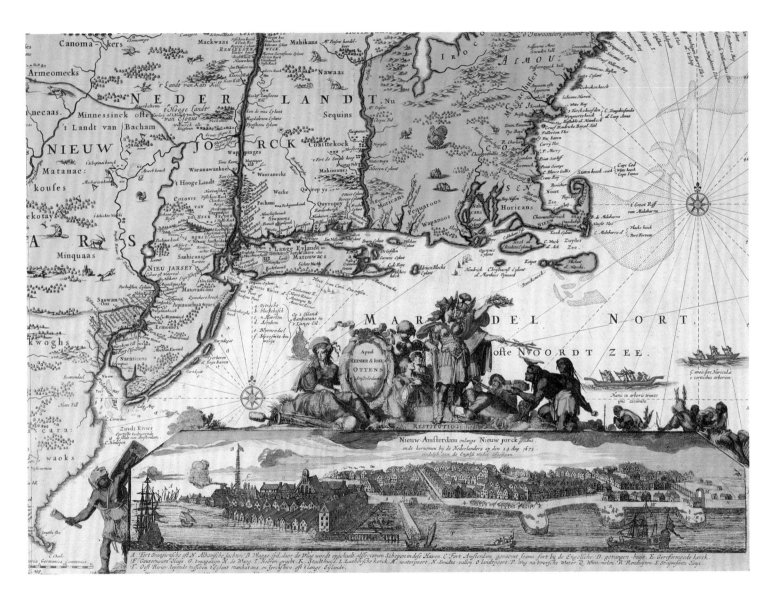

PLATE 5. *Totius Neobelgii accuratissima tabula.* "Restitution map" of New York,
showing the town after the Dutch recapture of 1673.

PLATE 6. Two butterfly species found in Suriname: the "Menelaus" (A and B) and the "Lavinia" (C and D). From Pieter Cramer, *De uitlandsche kapellen* (Amsterdam, 1779-1782).

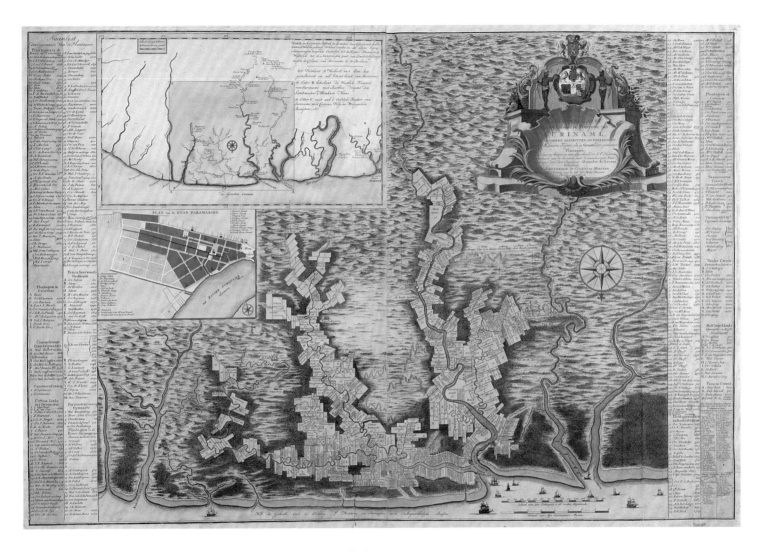

PLATE 7. A. de Lavaux, *Algemeene kaart van de colonie of provintie van Suriname*
(Amsterdam, after 1758), indicating both Suriname's plantations and the
communities formed by runaway slaves.

PLATE 8. A plantation in Suriname shortly before the Dutch abolished
slavery in 1863. From G.W.C. Voorduin, *Gezigten uit Neerland's West-Indien,
naar de natuur geteekend* (Amsterdam, 1860-1862).

FIG. 3.10 View of "Friburgum" or Vrijburg, the estate built by Governor Johan Maurits near Recife. From Caspar van Baerle, *Rerum per octennium in Brasilia* (Amsterdam, 1647).

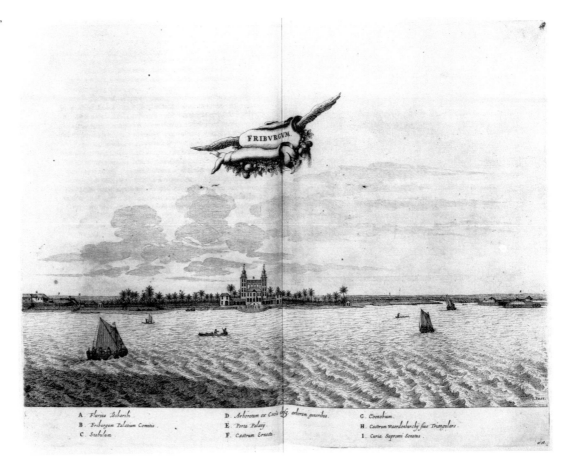

FIG. 3.11 Map of Vrijburg. From Caspar van Baerle, *Rerum per octennium in Brasilia* (Amsterdam, 1647).

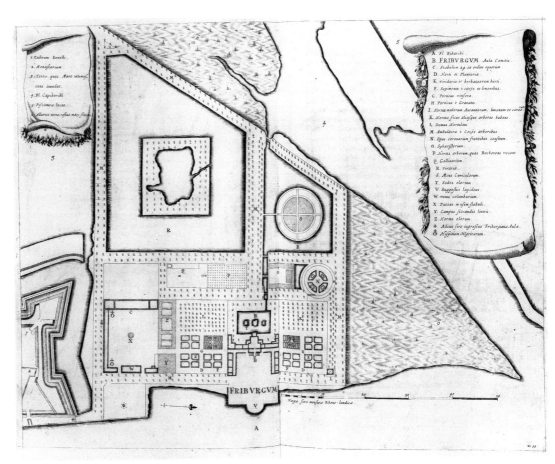

FIG. 3.12 Slaves in Dutch Brazil using calabashes as musical instruments, from Johan Nieuhof, *Gedenkweerdige Brasiliaense zee- en lant-reize* (Amsterdam, 1682).

FIG. 3.13 A native Brazilian archer killing a bird. Other natives are portrayed eating human flesh. From Johan Nieuhof, *Gedenkweerdige Brasiliaense zee- en lant-reize* (Amsterdam, 1682).

the Portuguese colonies in Africa, occupying Luanda and Benguela (which left him in control of the littoral of Angola), São Tomé, and the fort Axim in Guinea. A German soldier, Johann Paul Augspurger, took part in this expedition, which was again organized from New Holland. He gave his account of the mission in *Kurtze und warhaffte Beschreibung der See-Reisen von Amsterdam in Holland nacher Brasilien in America, und Angola in Africa* (Schleusingen, 1644) [**65**].[5] These conquests ensured the settlers in Brazil of a steady supply of slaves. During the twenty-four years of Dutch rule, over twenty-five thousand Africans were forcibly shipped to Brazil. This made the Dutch the leading slave traders in the Atlantic, despite the conviction of the local church consistory, unusual for the time, that slavery ran counter to justice.

While as a matter of principle Usselinx and others had objected to the introduction of slavery, because it was considered costly and because Africans were thought to work not nearly as hard as the Dutch

themselves, the small choir of protest fell silent once the economic benefits became clear. Yet the discussion did not cease altogether. In an influential book, *'t Geestelyck roer van 't coopmans schip* (Dordrecht, 1640) [**61**],[6] the minister Godfried Udemans (1580-1649) argued that Christians should not be enslaved, but Turks and heathens could be, provided that they were taken prisoner in a just, defensive war, or sold by their parents or other lawful masters for a fair price. Once instructed in the true faith, Udemans held, the slaves should be manumitted.

Udemans had in mind the Dutch in both the East and West Indies, but his reasoning could be applied also to the bondage of Indians in Brazil. The official Dutch position was that the freedom of indigenous peoples should be respected, a standpoint that the Company reiterated over and over again. In general,

---

5 "Short and true description of sea voyages from Amsterdam in Holland to Brazil in America, and Angola in Africa."

6 "The spiritual helm of the merchantman."

this served as a guiding principle, but still, during the short spell of Dutch rule in Maranhão, Indian slavery did exist. It was legitimized by the absence of black slaves and the prior Portuguese employment of Indian slaves in the area. Even in those areas of Brazil where Indians were not enslaved, the Dutch did have access to Indian labor, since many Indian village chiefs entered into contracts with employers.

For a long time, the war in Brazil went well. Johan Maurits forged ahead energetically by disposing of the guerrilla fighters to the north of the São Francisco River and annexing the district of Ceará, which meant that half of all the captaincies of Brazil were in Dutch hands. The governor now found it opportune to mount an attack on Bahia, Portugal's main bulwark in Brazil and a target of Dutch aggrandizement a decade earlier. With a force of 3,600 Europeans and 1,000 Indians, the Dutch captured the forts outside the town unopposed. But when fighting started in the city, the Portuguese held their own. Their numbers were superior, which gave the Portuguese defenders an edge, but even so, they barely won the battle. The next major encounter occurred in the waters near Recife, where Iberian forces also outnumbered the Dutch, three to one, and yet they could not win the battle. This deadlock was never afterwards overcome; the Netherlanders remained in Recife and the Iberians in Bahia.

American wars were a huge drain on Dutch funds. Even before Johan Maurits had set foot on Brazilian soil, the West India Company had run up a debt of eighteen million guilders, and this amount only increased in subsequent years. Economic hopes were placed on the sugar trade, but it faced some formidable obstacles. One was war itself. Plantations were destroyed in the course of it, and both sides availed themselves of scorched earth tactics. Another threat was posed by the Dunkirk privateers. Outgoing and returning ships between Dutch ports and Brazil were always at risk of being captured by these Flemish vessels in the employ of Spain. One merchant aboard a ship bound for Brazil, Gedeon Moris, experienced an exchange of fire with the Dunkirkers and told the story in his journal, which was then published [59].[7]

Even when sugar loads arrived safely in Dutch ports, the Company could not take full advantage of the success, because it had allowed its trade monopoly to be undermined. In fact, realizing that it lacked the working capital to pay for all imports from New Holland, the WIC had permitted a measure of free trade as early as 1630 [50].[8] When a reduction in freight rates led to increased returns to independent

merchants, the Company lodged a protest against the unseemly high profits made in a period of heavy warfare. To the dismay of the Amsterdam merchants outside of the Company, the States General now discontinued the free trade policy. The merchants pointed out that colonization would be impeded by a trade monopoly and argued that the Company would in fact gain from a thriving open trade by levying customs and freightage. These opinions were expressed in a true paper war: *Vertoogh by een lief-hebber des vaderlants vertoont. Teghen het ongefondeerde ende schadelijck sluyten der vryen handel in Brazil* (1637) [52];[9] *Bril-gesicht voor de verblinde eyghen baetsuchtige handelaers op Brasil* (1638) [54];[10] *Het spel van Brasilien, vergheleken by een goedt verkeer-spel* (1638) [55].[11]

Supported by Johan Maurits, the free trade lobbyists eventually carried the day; the monopoly came to an end after only a year and a half. The one concession the Amsterdam merchants had to make was that if they wanted to trade with Brazil, they were now all required to become shareholders of the Company [57].[12] The free traders were proven right in the next several years; their sugar imports were three times as high as those of the Company.

Nevertheless, WIC expenditures continued to exceed income by far, partly owing to the governor's prodigal spending, which may have underlain his recall in 1643. The official reason given was a military one. Four years before, after nearly sixty years of dominance by Spain, Portugal had risen in revolt, declaring itself an independent state. Soon afterwards, a truce with the United Provinces was concluded. The

---

7 Gedeon Moris, *Copye. Van 't journael gehouden by Gedeon Moris, koopman op het schip van de West-Indische Compagnie, genaemt de Princesse* ("Copy of the log kept by Gedeon Moris, merchant on the West India Company ship named the Princesse"). Amsterdam, 1640.

8 West-Indische Compagnie, *Articulen, met approbatie vande Ho: Mog: Heeren Staten Generael der Vereenichde Nederlanden, provisioneelijc beraemt* ("Provisonally planned articles, approved by the High Mightinesses the States General of the United Netherlands"). Amsterdam, 1631.

9 "Discourse by a devotee of the fatherland. Against the groundless and prejudicial implementation of free trade in Brazil."

10 "A pair of spectacles for the blinded, self-interested merchants trading with Brazil."

11 "The Brazil play, compared to a good game."

12 *Reglement byde UUest-Indische Compagnie, ter vergaderinge vande negentiene, met approbatie vande Ho: Mo: Heeren Staten Generael, over het openstellen vanden handel op Brazil provisioneel ghearresteert* ("Regulation regarding the opening of trade with Brazil, provisionally confirmed by the West India Company, during the meeting of the Nineteen [directors], and approved by the High Mightinesses the States General"). The Hague, 1638.

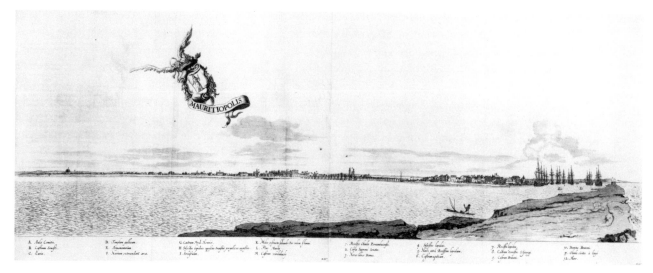

FIG. 3.14 Mauritiopolis or Mauritsstad, the capital of Dutch Brazil built by Johan Maurits. From Franciscus Plante, *Mauritiados* (Leiden, 1647).

FIG. 3.15 The skyline of Mauritsstad, Recife, and Olinda. From Matheus van den Broeck, *Journael ofte historiaelse beschrijvinge* (Amsterdam, 1651).

Nineteen at first awaited further developments but ultimately decided to reduce the garrison in Brazil and call back Johan Maurits. In May 1644, the Governor, Captain- and Admiral-General, as his official titles were, finally complied. The esteem in which he was held by the people was shown once again when the time came for his departure. Bursts of applause followed him when he rode to Paraíba to take ship. Accompanied by a hundred citizens on horseback, he found the road filled with people of all ranks and all ethnic backgrounds. When he finally reached the shore, a mob of Indians pushed the white men aside and carried him to the waiting vessel.

Tribute of another kind was paid to the "prince" by his learned chaplain, Frans Plante. His *Mauritiados* (Leiden, 1647), a poem of 6,430 hexameters [**75**], emulated Virgil's *Aeneid*. Mainly the relation of a succession of battles, according to the story a meeting of the gods sends Mercury to the Dutch, telling them they should teach the Spanish a lesson in the far west. Minerva persuades the other gods that the leader against the Spaniards should be Johan Maurits.

Resistance, Reaction, and Ruin

It was not long after Johan Maurits had departed that various problems began to arise. The governor had been able to address problems in time, or contain them, but once he was gone, Dutch government and the administration of justice were the target of criticism. Some years earlier, the Frenchman Auguste de Quelen, in a published work, had already questioned the underhanded dealings of the leadership, who took not the slightest notice of the guidelines provided by the WIC board [**60**].[13] Members of the central administration, the High Council, were denounced in other pamphlets for their alleged nepotism and their luxurious way of life: *De Brasilsche breede-byl; ofte t'samenspraek tusschen Kees Jansz. Schott, komende uyt Brasil, en Jan Maet, koopmans-knecht* (Amsterdam, 1647) [**72**];[14] *Brasilsche gelt-sack. Waer in dat claerlijck vertoont wordt waer dat de participanten van de West-Indische Comp. haer gelt ghebleven is* (1647) [**73**].[15]

The treatment of Portuguese citizens by Dutch officials was also exposed to much criticism. Van Quelen had singled out the fiscal officer and the bailiff, who by-passed normal court procedure by holding Portuguese citizens prisoner in their own houses and extorting money from them. In *Brasyls schuyt-praetjen* (1649) [**80**],[16] a fictitious conversation between an officer, a merchant, and a minister, other forms of malfeasance were revealed. In view of these abuses, it is hardly surprising that the Portuguese settlers rose up in rebellion, which

occurred unbeknownst to the authorities in Lisbon, although one pamphleteer accused the metropolitan government of complicity [**74**].[17] Shortly after the beginning of this uprising in June 1645, and carried by its momentum, many Dutch military posts in Pernambuco and Paraíba fell into the hands of the Portuguese [**68**],[18] [**70**].[19] One Dutch soldier who was taken captive, Matheus van den Broeck, later reported on his adventures in writing [**84**].[20] His booklet surely found ready buyers, for pamphlets containing the latest news were in demand [**78**].[21] How much the home front empathized with the overseas events was shown by an uproar in The Hague. The Prince of Orange and his regiments, with the assistance of garrisons from neighboring towns, barely succeeded in keeping a mob under control that tried to storm the residence of the Portuguese ambassador.

Reinforcements from the Netherlands, supplied by the States General, brought the total number of Dutch soldiers in Brazil to 5,000. The fresh troops arrived in the nick of time, since the Portuguese had already begun a siege of Recife. In April 1648, the Dutch commander Von Schoppe led an assault on the besiegers in the hills of the Guararapes, which

13 Auguste de Guelen, *Kort verhael vanden staet van Fernanbuc* ("Short narrative on the state of Pernambuco"). Amsterdam, 1640.

14 "The Brazilian broad axe or dialogue between Kees Jansz. Schott, coming from Brazil, and Jan Maet, merchant servant."

15 "Brazilian money-bag. In which is clearly shown where the money of the participants of the West India Company has gone."

16 "Brazilian boat talk."

17 *Claar vertooch van de verradersche en vyantlijcke acten en proceduren van Poortugaal, in 't verwecken ende stijven van de rebellie ende oorloghe in Brasil* ("Clear discourse on the treacherous and hostile acts and procedures of Portugal in generating and strengthening the rebellion and war in Brazil"). Amsterdam, 1647.

18 *Iournael ofte kort discours, nopende de rebellye ende verraderlycke desseynen der Portugesen* ("Journal or brief discourse regarding the rebellion and treacherous designs of the Portuguese"). Arnhem, 1647.

19 *Manifest door d'inwoonders van Parnambuco uytghegeven tot hun verantwoordinghe op 't aennemen der wapenen teghens de West-Indische Compagnie* ("Manifesto issued by the inhabitants of Pernambuco to account for taking up arms against the West India Company"). [Netherlands], 1646.

20 *Journael, ofte historiaelse beschrijvinge van Matheus vanden Broeck* ("Journal, or historical description of Matheus van den Broeck"). Amsterdam, 1651.

21 *Eenige advijsen ende verklaringhen uyt Brasilien* ("Some notices and declarations from Brazil"). Amsterdam [i.e. The Hague], 1648.

FIG. 3.16 In July 1645, 1,000 Portuguese rebels, led by João Fernandes Vieira, attacked the sugar mill of the Dutchman Aernout de Landa. From Matheus van den Broeck, *Journael, ofte historiaelse beschrijvinge* (Amsterdam, 1651).

ended in a humiliating defeat. Five hundred Dutchmen lost their lives. The outcome of the next major engagement, which took place in the same setting before a year had passed, was even worse: 957 fell victim, among them 100 officers.

Dutch successes were now confined to the high seas. Within a few years time, privateers from Zeeland seized over 200 vessels plying between Brazil and Portugal, which had a deleterious effect on the Portuguese budget. Lisbon's countermaneuver was to found a company, modelled on the West India Company, with the responsibility of fitting out eighteen war ships to convoy the sugar fleets. In exchange, the company was granted extensive trading privileges. The company turned out to be well-conceived and took the sting out of Zeeland privateering.

In 1648 the United Provinces signed the peace treaty of Munster with Spain, which meant that troops and funds became available to back up the hard-pressed West India Company. Admiral Witte de With was promptly sent with twelve warships to Rio de Janeiro to overwhelm a sugar fleet. Lack of victuals forced De With to sail for Recife, however, and the Portuguese fleet was able to leave without hindrance. The details of this aborted expedition can be found in the account of Nicolaus de Graaff, who served as a surgeon on one of the ships [125].[22]

All through this epoch, the war-weary Portuguese King João IV was flirting with the idea of abandoning Pernambuco and handing it over to the Dutch. In 1653, however, he found new resolve and decided to try an attack on Recife by sea. The timing was right, since the Dutch garrison had lost all motivation. Only two weeks prior to the attack, commander Von Schoppe was complaining that many of his soldiers had served for over a decade and were on the verge of despair. Another problem was that many of the new recruits were much too young [88].[23] Von Schoppe's letter was addressed to the States General, but it arrived too late. On January 26, 1654 the Portuguese forced the High Council to surrender. The capitulation left behind a bitter taste of failure [89],[24] [90].[25]

22 *Reisen van Nicolaus de Graaff, na de vier gedeeltens des werelds, als Asia, Africa, America en Europa* ("Travels of Nicolaus de Graaff to the four parts of the world, Asia, Africa, America, and Europe"). Hoorn, 1701.

23 *Copie, van den brief geschreven by Sigismund van Shoppe* [sic] ("Copy of the letter, written by Sigismund van Schoppe"). Middelburg, 1654.

24 *Accoord van Brasilien, mede van 't Recif, Maurits-Stadt, ende de omleggende forten van Brasil* ("Agreement of Brazil, including Recife, Mauritsstad, and the neighboring forts of Brazil"). Amsterdam, 1654.

25 *Cort, bondigh ende waerachtigh verhael van 't schandelijck overgeven ende verlaten vande voorname conquesten van Brasil* ("Brief, concise and honest story about the outrageous surrender and abandonment of the principal conquests of Brazil"). Middelburg, 1655.

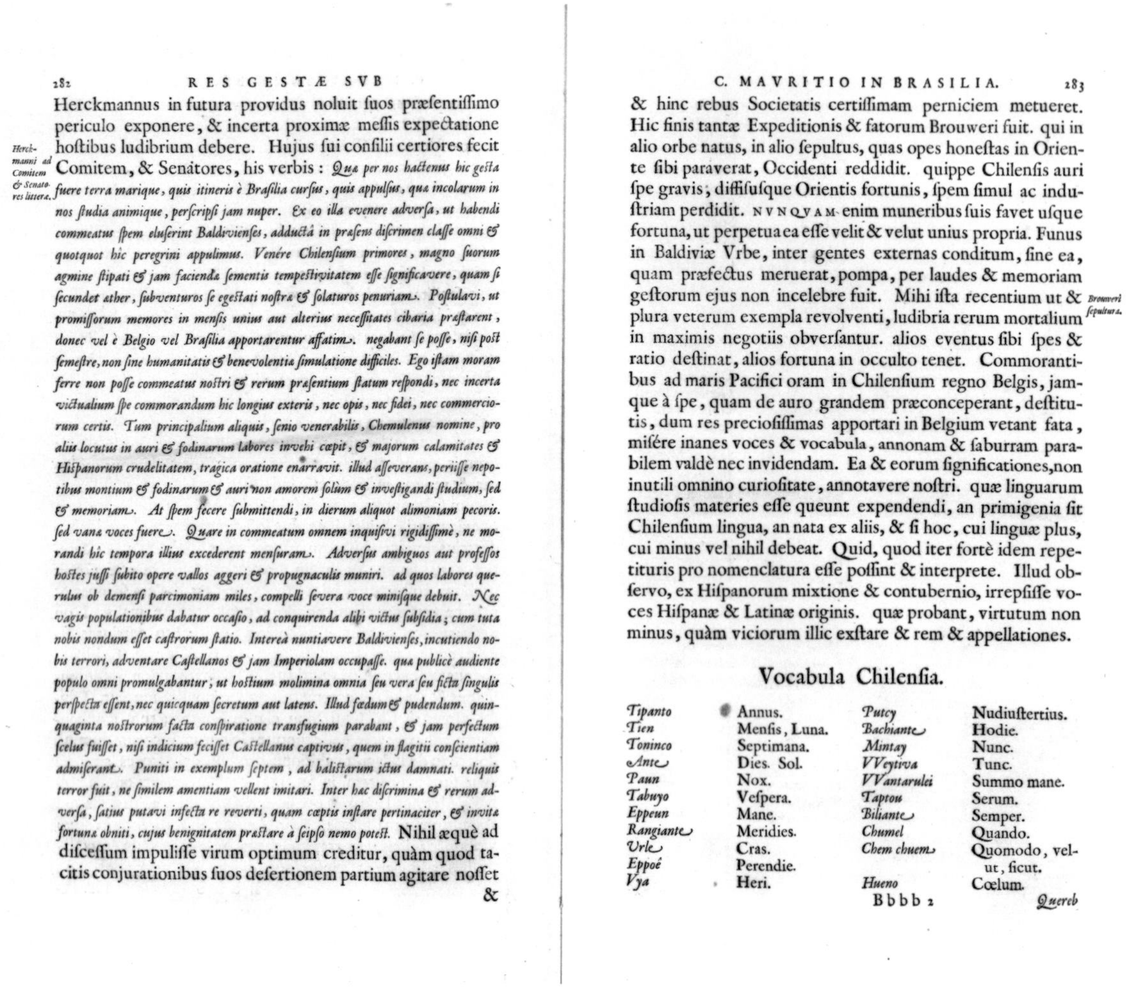

Herckmanni ad Comitem & Senatores literæ.

Herckmannus in futura providus noluit suos præsentissimo periculo exponere, & incerta proximæ messis expectatione hostibus ludibrium debere. Hujus sui consilii certiores fecit Comitem, & Senatores, his verbis : *Quæ per nos hactenus hic gesta fuere terra marique, quis itineris è Brasilia cursus, quis appulsus, quæ incolarum in nos studia animique, perscripsi jam nuper. Ex eo illa evenere adversa, ut habendi commeatus spem eluserint Baldivienses, adducta in præsens discrimen classe omni & quotquot hic peregrini appulimus. Venére Chilensium primores, magno suorum agmine stipati & jam facienda sementi tempestivitatem esse significavere, quam si secundet æther, subventuros se egestati nostræ & solaturos penuriam. Postulavi, ut promissorum memores in mensis unius aut alterius necessitates cibaria præstarent, donec vel è Belgio vel Brasilia apportarentur affatim. negabant se posse, nisi post semestre, non sine humanitate & benevolentiæ simulatione difficiles. Ego istam moram ferre non posse commeatus nostri & rerum præsentium statum respondi, nec incerta victualium spe longius exteris, nec opis, nec fidei, nec commerciorum certis. Tum principalium aliquis, senio venerabilis, Chemulenus nomine, pro aliis locutus in auri & fodinarum labores invehi cæpit, & majorum calamitates & Hispanorum crudelitatem, tragica oratione enarravit. illud asseverans, periisse nepotibus montium & fodinarum & auri non amorem solum & investigandi studium, sed & memoriam. At spem fecere submittendi, in dierum aliquot alimoniam pecoris. sed vana voces fuere. Quare in commeatum omnem inquisivi rigidissime, ne morandi hic tempora illius excederent mensuram. Adversus ambiguos aut professos hostes jussi subito opere vallos aggeri & propugnaculis muniri. ad quos labores querulus ob demensi parcimoniam miles, compelli severa voce minusque debuit. Nec vagis populationibus dabatur occasio, ad conquirenda alibi victui subsidia; cum tuta nobis nondum esset castrorum statio. Interea nuntiavere Baldivienses, incutiendo nobis terrori, adventare Castellanos & jam Imperiolam occupasse. qua publice audiente populo omni promulgabantur, ut hostium molimina omnia seu vera seu ficta singulis perspecta & vera essent, nec quicquam secretum aut latens. Illud fœdum & pudendum. quinquaginta nostrorum facta conspiratione transfugium parabant, & jam perfectum scelus fuisset, nisi indicium fecisset Castellanus captivus, quem in flagitii conscientiam admiserant. Puniti in exemplum septem, ad balistarum ictum damnati. reliqui terror fuit, ne similem amentiam vellent imitari. Inter hæc discrimina & rerum adversa, satius putavi infecta re reverti, quam cæptis instare pertinaciter, & invita fortuna obniti, cujus benignitatem præstare à seipso nemo potest.* Nihil æque ad discessum impulisse virum optimum creditur, quam quod tacitis conjurationibus suos defectionem partium agitare nosset

&

& hinc rebus Societatis certissimam perniciem metueret. Hic finis tantæ Expeditionis & fatorum Brouweri fuit. qui in alio orbe natus, in alio sepultus, quas opes honestas in Oriente sibi paraverat, Occidenti reddidit. quippe Chilensis auri spe gravis, diffisusque Orientis fortunis, spem simul ac industriam perdidit. NVNQVAM enim muneribus suis favet usque fortuna, ut perpetua ea esse velit & velut unius propria. Funus in Baldiviæ Vrbe, inter gentes externas conditum, sine ea, quam præfectus meruerat, pompa, per laudes & memoriam gestorum ejus non incelebre fuit. Mihi ista recentiora ut & *Brouweri sepultura.* plura veterum exempla revolventi, ludibria rerum mortalium in maximis negotiis obversantur. alios eventus sibi spes & ratio destinat, alios fortuna in occulto tenet. Commorantibus ad maris Pacifici oram in Chilensium regno Belgis, jamque à spe, quam de auro grandem præconceperant, destitutis, dum res preciosissimas apportari in Belgium vetant fata, misére inanes voces & vocabula, annonam & saburram parabilem valde nec invidendam. Ea & eorum significationes, non inutili omnino curiositate, annotavere nostri. quæ linguarum studiosis materies esse queunt expendendi, an primigenia sit Chilensium lingua, an nata ex aliis, & si hoc, cui linguæ plus, cui minus vel nihil debeat. Quid, quod iter forte idem repetituris pro nomenclatura esse possint & interprete. Illud observo, ex Hispanorum mixtione & contubernio, irrepsisse voces Hispanæ & Latinæ originis. quæ probant, virtutum non minus, quàm viciorum illic exstare & rem & appellationes.

Vocabula Chilensia.

Tipanto	Annus.	Putcy	Nudiustertius.
Tien	Mensis, Luna.	Bachiante	Hodie.
Toninco	Septimana.	Mintay	Nunc.
Ante	Dies. Sol.	VVeytiva	Tunc.
Paun	Nox.	VVantarulei	Summo mane.
Tabuyo	Vespera.	Taptou	Serum.
Eppeun	Mane.	Biliante	Semper.
Rangiante	Meridies.	Chumel	Quando.
Vrle	Cras.	Chem chuem	Quomodo, vel- ut, ficut.
Eppoé	Perendie.		
Vya	Heri.	Hueno	Cœlum.

Bbbb 2   Qnereb

FIG. 3.18   An expedition in 1643-44 aimed at the conquest of Chile ended in failure. One of the few gains was the information gathered on the native language of the area. From Caspar van Baerle, *Rerum per octennium in Brasilia* (Amsterdam, 1647).

A Curious Expedition to Chile

New Holland was still in its infancy when a number of Dutch ships set off in 1642 on an expedition to conquer Chile. In the years leading up to the foundation of the West India Company there had been much talk about colonizing the elongated Spanish province, which could serve as a base of operations from the West against coastal Peru and New Spain. Chile was also valued for its good farming land and gold mines. The Dutch had become acquainted with Chile initially in their series of voyages through the Strait of Magellan, but their colonization plans were postponed for several decades. It was only during a lull in the fighting in Brazil that a serious effort at conquest could be initiated. The expeditionary naval force sailed from the Netherlands first to Brazil, where it was reinforced with several ships, and the whole fleet left Recife in January, 1643. In charge of the expedition was Hendrik Brouwer (1581-1643), a former Governor-General of the Dutch East Indies. His account of the voyage was later published as *Journael ende historis verhael vande reyse gedaen by oosten de straet le Maire, naer de custen van Chili* (Amsterdam, 1646) [**69**].[26]

Having rounded Cape Horn, Brouwer and his men arrived at Chiloé and from there passed to the continent. Contacts were established with the Araucanian Indians and plans made to fight the common enemy: Spain. A Dutch base was set up in Valdivia and for a moment, the prospects seemed good. In the end, however, the expedition failed dis-

---

26 "Journal and historical story about the voyage made east of Strait le Maire, to the coast of Chile."

mally. The Indians, who were essential to the strategy, could not be persuaded to form an alliance, and the Dutch soon ran short of provisions. Brouwer himself did not survive the mission, and the only real gain was the discovery that a wide passage separated Staten Land from Antarctica, the "Southland." Though it was found by Brouwer, the passage has come to be known as Drake Strait.

The Old Company and the New

In Dutch public opinion, almost no year went by without the West India Company being heavily criticized. The *Discours op verscheyde voorslaghen rakende d'Oost en UUest-Indische trafyken* (1645) [**67**][27] charged that the Company had squandered its financial means but still been unable to conquer the silver-rich countries of Peru and New Spain. The *Amsterdamsche veerman op Middelburgh* (Flushing, 1650) [**82**][28] insinuated that a number of Company directors were guilty of dubious legal practices.

Financial problems seemed to invite desperate solutions. For a long time, negotiations were carried on that were meant to result in a merger with the much more successful VOC. In *Aenwysinge: Datmen vande Oost en West-Indische Compagnien een compangie* [sic] *dient te maken* (The Hague, 1644) [**64**][29] a few options were suggested. The East India Company eventually managed to avert an amalgamation by donating 1.5 million guilders to its needy sister [**86**].[30]

The loss of "New Holland" compounded the existing problems and nearly dealt a deathblow to the WIC. Most of its funds had been used to make the colonization of Brazil a success. Large sums of money were invested in the development of the sugar industry, including, for years on end, the sale of slaves on credit to the Portuguese planters. Only a small fraction of these outstanding debts—amounting to millions of guilders—would ever be paid off. Moreover, the cost of the military efforts to retain Brazil made awesome inroads on the Company treasury. During this same period, the Company also lost control of New Amsterdam. The WIC directors managed to prolong the Company's existence by issuing bonds and entering into bottomry contracts, obligations which stipulated that the debtor pledge as collateral either his ship or the cargo or both. Even so, in 1674 the curtain came down.

Simultaneously with the old Company's dissolution, a new one was founded which was expressly not charged with war tasks but was set up as a purely commercial company. Old debts and shares were turned into new ones, by which means the new WIC acquired share capital of 6.3 million and working capital of 1.2 million guilders. To cut back on the Company's expenses, the number of directors of the various Chambers was reduced by half, while the board of nineteen governors was replaced by one of ten.

The prospects of the new WIC could not be compared with those of its predecessor. A lot had changed in the intermediate half-century. The first Company had been established in an optimistic era which saw the supremacy of Dutch trade. The second Company, however, was set up when stadholder William III, the future king of England, had barely succeeded in saving his country from ruin. In 1672 a third Anglo-Dutch war had broken out, but even more serious was the simultaneous eastern invasion of troops from Cologne and Munster and the invasion of Louis XIV's army. Survival of the United Provinces under these pressures was nearly miraculous. Illustrative of Dutch decline was the modest size of the settlements the new West India Company ruled in the Americas. Twenty years after the loss of New Holland and a decade after the English conquest of New Netherland, the Dutch "empire" consisted only of six Caribbean islands, the former English colony of Suriname, and a string of small Guiana settlements.

---

27 "Discourse on various proposals regarding East- and West-Indian shipping traffic."
28 "The Amsterdam ferryman to Middelburg."
29 "Proof that one ought to make one company out of the East and West India Companies."
30 *Vertoogh, over den toestant der West-Indische Compagnie* ("Discourse on the state of the West India Company"). Rotterdam, 1651.

FIG. 4.1 Pelicans, a penguin, a raven and other American animal species from Simon de Vries, *Curieuse aenmerckingen der bysonderste Oost en West-Indische verwonderens-waerdige dingen* (Utrecht, 1682).

CHAPTER 4

Images and Knowledge
of the New World

FIG. 4.2 The armadillo was often used as a symbol of the New World. From Hendrick Ottsen, *Iournael oft daghelijcx-register* (Amsterdam, 1617).

News of the fabulous wealth of the Americas did not fail to impress Netherlanders. Some even had the privilege of beholding the riches from the New World with their own eyes. As early as 1520, only one year after Cortés had entered "New Spain" near Veracruz, the finest Mexican weapons, suits of armor and shields, as well as a golden sun and a silver moon were already displayed in Brussels. The great German artist Albrecht Dürer could hardly believe what he saw.

It was Dürer himself who had sought to represent the European continent in a single fetching image. Adapting a Greek myth, he painted the abduction of the virgin Europa by Jupiter, who for the occasion had taken the shape of a white bull. According to Ovid's story, Jupiter took Europa to Crete, where he begot children by her that became the Europeans. The single image the Old World later created to typify the New owed a lot to Dürer. In 1594, Maarten de Vos from Antwerp conceived of America as a nude Indian girl riding a giant armadillo, that uniquely and exotic American animal. This image stuck. In 1617 the picture of a martial Indian in an exotic landscape seated on an armadillo embellished the cover of a Dutch travel account dealing with the Río de la Plata [23], and it appeared frequently thereafter as a symbol of the newly discovered continents of the Western Hemisphere.

Printed information about the New World was available in Dutch from the beginning of the sixteenth century. A Dutch translation of Amerigo Vespucci's letter to Lorenzo de' Medici, describing his third voyage to America, was published in Antwerp in 1507 [1].[1] The Dutch version is derived from a Latin translation of the Italian original. As an important center of book production, the Netherlands was a good place to live if one was eager to receive information about the New World. Between 1500 and 1610, 30,000 titles were published there, which may be equated with 30,000,000 copies. A good number of these titles would have American references in them. In the private libraries of intellectuals from the northern Netherlands, numerous works on the Americas could be found. The most popular book was José de Acosta's *Historia natural y moral de las Indias*, originally published in 1590.

After the outbreak of war with Spain in 1568, the Dutch image of the Americas underwent a profound

---

1 *Van der nieuwer werelt oft landtscap nieuwelicx gheuo[n]de[n] va[n] de[n] doorluchtighe[n] con[inc]. van Portugael door den alder beste[n] pyloet ofte zeekender d[er] werelt* ("On the new world or landscape recently found for the serene king of Portugal by the best pilot or explorer in the world").

Figuere Num. 16.

Siet hier het Spaenſch gebroet de Indianen kneuſen,
Berooven en ontleen van Handen, Oogen, Neuſen,
O jammerlijcke daedt! mijn Hert ſchrickt in mijn Borſt,
En vloeckt den Schellem die dit eerſtmael droomen dorſt;
Wat helſche Tyranny, wat verduyvelde vonden:
De weerelooſe Swart gejaecght werdt van de Honden.
Het gheen de Nicker nau ſou dencken of vermoen,
Dat durft een Spangiaert ſtout gantſch God-vergeten doen.
L 2   Op

FIG. 4.3 The Dutch propaganda machine produced numerous illustrations like this one from Bartolomé de las Casas, *Den spieghel der Spaense tyrannye* (Amsterdam, 1638), showing Spaniards mutilating Indians during the conquest of New Granada.

change. Depicting the war as a moral conflict, Dutch pamphleteers did not stop short of exaggeration, even though the reality was itself shocking enough. Spanish massacres, for instance, took place in the towns of Naarden and Malines. In their descriptions of the events, the Dutch typically passed over the fact that the majority of the so-called "Spanish" troops were mere enlistees from the northern and southern Netherlands. Moreover, the Dutch for their part committed atrocities as well. What the pamphleteers emphasized, however, was the alleged *inherent* Spanish cruelty and despotism, an assessment based on the merging of the worst that could be said about Spain's conduct in both the Low Countries and America. Spanish pride, mendacity, avarice and other vices were recurrent themes in writings such as William the Silent's frequently reprinted *Apologie* (1581). These sixteenth-century pamphlets began a

literary tradition that historians since the early twentieth century have called the Black Legend, a tradition intended to malign Spain and the Spaniards, which has spanned several centuries, travelled all across Europe, and to some degree still has life in it.

The impression that the Duke of Alba had come to the Netherlands not simply to enforce government measures, but rather to conquer and colonize, was closely linked to a biased account of Spanish actions in the Americas. What the Spaniards had done to the Indians might very well be what was awaiting the Dutch. Gradually, through the force of this writing, the New World came to be viewed as a continent of hellish torment, where most of what the Spaniards did was to kill natives and overpower the survivors in the cruelest of ways [29].[2]

In this context, the most damaging indictment of all ironically came from the hands of a Spaniard: the lament of Bartolomé de Las Casas, a Dominican friar and self-appointed advocate of the Indians whose exertions ultimately resulted in the abolition of Indian slavery. The Las Casas work that was most useful for the Dutch rebels was his *Brevíssima Relación de la Destrucción de las Indias*. Published in 1552, the book was widely translated and went through many Dutch editions. The first of these was *Seer cort verhael vande destructie van d'Indien* (Antwerp?, 1578) [3].[3] Soon, it was not enough simply for the Dutch to read in their own language about Spanish misdeeds; graphic illustrations, too, were required. These were supplied by Théodore de Bry, an artist from the southern Netherlands, as embellishments to Las Casas' text. Poems were inserted as captions to the pictures, such as the verses of Gerbrand Adriaensz. Bredero, one of the greatest Dutch writers and poets. A Las Casas edition of 1638 added new Spanish cruelties, committed in France and the Low Countries [53].[4]

Although the Black Legend literary tradition may have diminished after the Dutch-Spanish war, it cer-

---

2 Johannes Avontroot, *Den grouwel der verwoestinghe oft grondich bericht ende ontdeckinghe, van de gronden der Spaensche Inquisitie* ("The terror of destruction, or a searching examination and disclosure of the foundations of the Spanish Inquisition"). The Hague, 1621.

3 "Very short account of the destruction of the Indies."

4 *Den spieghel der Spaense tyrannye geschiet in West-Indien. Waer in te sien is de onmenschelicke wreede feyten der Spangiaerden, met t'samen de beschrijvinghe der selver landen, volckeren aert ende nature* ("The Mirror of Spanish Tyranny exercised in the West Indies. In which are shown the inhuman cruel acts of the Spaniards, along with the description of those Lands, Peoples and their nature"). Amsterdam, 1638.

FIG. 4.4 Spreading death and destruction here are Pedro de Alvarado and his men during the conquest of Guatemala. From Simon de Vries, *Curieuse aenmerckingen der bijsonderste Oost en West-Indische verwonderenswaerdige dingen* (Utrecht, 1682).

FIG. 4.5 This idyllic depiction of Precolumbian life contrasted sharply with the everyday cruelties Dutch authors ascribed to the invading Spanish armies. From Arnoldus Montanus, *De nieuwe en onbekende weereld* (Amsterdam, 1671).

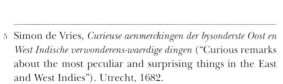

FIG. 4.6 J. Nomsz, *Bartholomeus Las Casas* (Amsterdam, 1785). In this Dutch play, set in a desert near Panama, a native princess falls in love with the son of a bloodthirsty Spanish commander. She trusts in the Christian God and the Gospel that is preached by Bartolomé de Las Casas, shown on the left here.

tainly did not disappear. Dutch eagerness to dish up stories of Spaniards engaged in atrocities continued apace. In a 1682 anthology of curious anecdotes from around the world, the cruelties of Pedro de Alvarado and his men, the conquerors of Guatemala, were portrayed in keeping with Las Casas' description. A public slaughterhouse is shown in Alvarado's army camp, where small children were roasted and human flesh was for sale [**118**].[5]

In the last quarter of the eighteenth century, the Black Legend was the leitmotiv in a series of Dutch plays put into verse and set in the Americas at the time of the conquest. One such play deplores the fate of the Indian Monzongo, who was once king of Veragua but is now slave to Hernán Cortés on Hispaniola [**145**].[6] Another has as its setting the court of "Ataliba, the supreme Inca of Quito," and tells the story of a Spanish nobleman who feels remorse for the conduct of his countrymen and starts to train the Inca armies "in a European manner" [**156**].[7] Yet another book highlights the adventures of Don Gonzalves Davila, a Spanish captain

---

5 Simon de Vries, *Curieuse aenmerckingen der bysonderste Oost en West Indische verwonderens-waerdige dingen* ("Curious remarks about the most peculiar and surprising things in the East and West Indies"). Utrecht, 1682.

6 Nicolaas Simon van Winter, *Monzongo, of De koninglyke slaaf. Treurspel* ("Monzongo, or the royal slave. Tragedy"). Amsterdam, 1774.

7 J. Nomsz, *Cora, of de Peruanen* ("Cora, or the Peruvians"). Amsterdam, 1784.

and the son of the commanding officer of Panama, Don Pedro Arias Davila. Davila Jr. and Emire, the daughter of an exiled Indian prince from Panama, fall in love despite the fact that Davila Sr. burned Emire's mother alive and although the Spaniards let their dogs devour her brother and tortured her father to find gold. Emire forgives her lover because she trusts the Christian philosophy preached on the spot by Las Casas himself [**157**].[8]

The New World according to De Laet

While in the sixteenth century the Americas had remained a place the Netherlanders learned about mainly through hearsay, in the next century an increasing number of Dutchmen could report about the New World from their own observations. Initially, Dutch voyages across the Atlantic depended on the dead reckoning of the ship's captains, since determining longitude at sea was still a puzzle and reliable charts were rare. In 1623, however, Dierick Ruyters published *Toortse der zeevaart*,[9] the long-awaited navigator's manual for the southern Atlantic, based on the work of the famous cosmographer Manuel de Figueiredo and other Portuguese accounts, as well as Ruyters' own experience. The book was particularly useful for shipping traffic to Africa but contained information also on the sea lanes to the Caribbean and Brazil, where Ruyters had once been a prisoner and where he later served as a ship's commander in the Dutch invasion of 1630.

In 1625, another fundamental Dutch work was brought out concerning the Americas: *Nieuvve wereldt ofte beschrijvinghe van West-Indien* [**37**][10] by Johannes de Laet. De Laet (Antwerp, 1581-1649) had participated in the Synod of Dordrecht on the Contra-Remonstrant side and was a director of the West India Company. A man of wide reading, he wrote booklets on Spain, France, the United Provinces, Turkey, the Empire of the Grand Mogul, Persia, Portugal, and Poland. To prepare for his work on the New World, he interviewed Dutch seamen and reviewed virtually all the existing books on the subject in all languages. The outcome was less alluring than Linschoten's *Itinerario* [**5**], but it was a more informative book with its clear sailing instructions and coastal charts. Five years later, in 1630, an improved version came out, and soon translations followed in Latin and French. De Laet later assumed the role of WIC historian with his four-volume *Historie ofte Iaerlijck verhael van de verrichtingen der Geoctroyeerde West-Indische Compagnie* (Leyden, 1644) [**66**].[11] In this work the Company's operations, especially in Brazil, are described in meticulous detail.

In the 1640s, a debate broke out between De Laet and one of the foremost Dutch scholars of all time, the jurist and theologian Hugo Grotius (1583-1645). Grotius earned lasting renown for his work *De iure belli ac pacis*, which laid the foundations of international and modern natural law. During the Twelve-Year Truce, he had been arrested for his Remonstrant views, but he eluded a life sentence in jail by escaping—hidden in a book trunk—from the castle where he was detained and crossing the German border disguised as a bricklayer.

His argument with Johannes de Laet concerned the origins of the native Americans [**62**],[12] [**63**].[13] Grotius advanced the view that all North American Indians descended from Scandinavian voyagers, with the exception of the people of Yucatán, whom Grotius considered to be the offspring of Ethiopian Christians. The ancestors of the South American Indians, Grotius believed, were migrated Indonesians and South Sea dwellers.

More or less reiterating the ideas put forward earlier by José de Acosta, De Laet, on the other hand, defended the theory that people from northeast Asia had come to the Americas across the Bering Strait and that the Indians were their descendants. Grotius's idea about the relationship between the South Americans, especially those in the vicinity of the Strait of Magellan, and the Indonesians, was shared by at least one group of Dutch explorers, for when the expedition of Schouten and Le Maire came upon a group of Indians near the Juan Fernández Islands (to the west of central Chile), the adventurers expressed surprise to find that none spoke Dutch, Spanish, Malay, or Javanese.

Aside from the speculation generated by the question of origins, there was a growing body of literature on other matters that took on a more or less anthropological bias. A hint of cultural relativism can be detected, for instance, in *Pertinente beschrijvinge van Guiana. Gelegen aan de vaste kust van America*

---

8 J. Nomsz, *Bartholomeus Las Casas.* Amsterdam, 1785.
9 "Torch of navigation."
10 "New World or description of the West Indies."
11 "History or yearly narrative of the actions of the patented West India Company".
12 *Hugonis Grotii De origine gentium Americanarum dissertatio altera, adversus obtrectatorem* ("Another treatise by Hugo Grotius on the origins of the American peoples"). Paris, 1643.
13 *Ioannis de Laet Antwerpiani Notae ad dissertationem Hugonis Grotii De origine gentium Americanarum* ("Critical remarks by Joannes de Laet of Antwerp on the treatise of Hugo Grotius on the origins of the American peoples"). Amsterdam, 1643.

POTOSI.

FIG. 4.7 A fanciful depiction of Potosí in Upper Peru, the center of
silver mining in South America. From Arnoldus Montanus, *De nieuwe
en onbekende weereld* (Amsterdam, 1671).

(Amsterdam, 1676) [**112**].[14] It held up the social life of the Carib Indians as an example for European "princes, states and monarchies." Whereas the European custom was to offer rewards for services rendered, the basic principle of Carib society was "to reward according to merits, to repay efforts, and to punish evil properly."

A book whose title was reminiscent of, and whose quality was in no way inferior to, De Laet's work was Arnoldus Montanus's *De Nieuwe en onbekende Weereld: of beschryving van America en 't Zuid-Land* (Amsterdam, 1671) [**106**].[15] This learned book, whose authorship has also been attributed to Olfert Dapper, includes theories about the origin of the Americans, voyages of discovery, and descriptions of towns and villages. Its solidity was marred only by somewhat fanciful illustrations. Montanus's paragraph on the famous silver mines of Potosí in the Spanish viceroyalty of Peru details the use of horse-mills and watermills to process the silver. The illustrator of the volume erroneously associated typical Dutch windmills with the ones described in the text.

A Great Mapmaking Tradition

Little is known about Arnoldus Montanus, apart from his close connections to the Dutch mapmaking tradition. His maternal grandfather, Jodocus Hondius, Sr., and his father, Petrus Montanus, were both members of the select company of Flemish cartographers in Amsterdam.

Aside from this Flemish school, a Holland school of cartography also emerged in the early seventeenth century, rooted in two traditions: on the one hand, the editing of maritime maps, guides, and journals, and on the other, the painting of richly decorated parchment sea maps. The indisputable leader of the Holland school was Willem Jansz. Blaeu (1571-1638). A student of the famous Danish astronomer Tycho Brahe, Blaeu was a man of many talents. He improved the printing press, he was an outstanding globe-maker and made considerable advances in the field of geodesy, but first and foremost he was a leading cartographer. In 1633, Willem was appointed the official cartographer of the Dutch East India Company, but his map of the Americas, published in his *Tweede deel van 't Tooneel des aerdriicx* (Amsterdam, 1635) [**51**][16] remains a classic. For this one achievement, however, Hessel Gerritsz should be given at least as much credit as Blaeu. Gerritsz had taken part in expeditions to Brazil and the Caribbean, and the accurate charts in De Laet's *Nieuvve wereldt* [**37**] were his work. Acting in close conjunction with Plancius, it was he who directed the hydrographic office of the West India Company, where all the latest information was collected. Ships' captains serving the Company were required to hand in their charts, maps, and journals upon returning home, and with this data the maps were continuously improved and brought up-to-date.

Beginning in the 1630s, the Blaeu company eclipsed the Hondius firm and all others in Europe in the atlas market. After the death of Willem Blaeu, his son Joan Sr. (1596-1673) assumed control, and under his direction the Blaeu printery achieved immortal fame in the world of publishing for the historical, theological, and literary works coming off its press. The printing establishment tragically burned to the ground in 1672, but fortunately not before the completion in 1662 of the Latin edition of the *Atlas Major* [**98**], an eleven-volume folio world atlas containing six hundred plates. Other editions appeared in French, Dutch, German, and Spanish. For three years, eight compositors were working full-time on the French, Dutch, and Latin editions only, with nine presses running simultaneously. The frontispiece of the volume dealing with the Americas was a magnificent allegory. Only four maps were specially engraved for this volume; the rest were reprints of earlier Blaeu issues.

In this golden age of Dutch cartography, the profile of New Amsterdam (New York) engraved around 1651 by Pieter Schut, an assistant of Claes Jansz. Visscher, deserves special mention. It is considered the earliest printed view of New York City [**87**].[17]

Just as the Blaeu company had triumphed over its principal competitor, the firm of Hondius, so it was now itself overtaken by Johannes van Keulen (1654-1715) and company. Van Keulen purchased many printed and drawn maps and charts from his rival Blaeu after the great fire. But after Van Keulen's decease, the leading position of the Dutch in cartography began to erode. Eventually, the skill and marketing of English and French mapmakers came to outstrip the Dutch.

The growth and dissemination of Dutch knowledge of America, nonetheless, was not halted. Despite the loss of Brazil in 1654 and the scientific establishment there, the plant and animal life of the New World continued to attract scholarly attention.

---

14 "Pertinent description of Guiana. Located on the mainland of America."

15 "The new and unknown world: or description of America and the Southland."

16 "Second part of the Theatre of the world."

17 Nicolaes Visscher, *Novi Belgii, Novaeque Angliae nec non partis Virginiae tabula*. Amsterdam, ca. 1651.

FIG. 4.8 Engraved title-page from Simon de Vries, *Curieuse aenmerckingen der bysonderste Oost en West Indische verwonderens-waerdige dingen* (Utrecht, 1682), a collection of curious stories from the non-European world.

FIG. 4.9 Scenes from Virginia and Brazil. In the middle, a group of Virginian Indians is having a bath, while in the forefront a Tapuya Indian from Brazil and a group of cannibals are preparing meals. From Simon de Vries, *Curieuse aenmerckingen der bijsonderste Oost en West-Indische verwonderens-waerdige dingen* (Utrecht, 1682).

The naturalist Aernout Vosmaer (1720-1799), for example, assembled a private collection of 15,000 natural history specimens. The plates in his *Natuurkundige beschryving eener uitmuntende verzameling van zeldsaame gedierten, bestaande in Oost- en Westindische viervoetige dieren, vogelen en slangen* (Amsterdam, 1804) [**167**][18] show what were then largely unknown animals. His description of the natural world of the Dutch colonies included Surinamese snakes, monkeys, and a wide variety of other animals. Probably because Suriname was home to an almost infinite variety of butterflies, the Dutch became the leading scholars in this field of natural history. In the 1680s, publications by scholars such as Stephanus Blankaart opened up this field, which was further developed by the remarkable German painter and naturalist Maria Sibylla Merian (1647-1717). Her stay in the colony between

1699 and 1701 led to the publication of the sumptuous folio *Dissertatio de generatione et metamorphosibus insectorum Surinamensium* (Amsterdam, 1719) [**132**].[19] Surinamese butterflies also filled the pages of Peter Cramer's lavishly illustrated *De uitlandsche kapellen voorkomende in de drie Waereld-deelen Asia, Africa en America*, published many years later (1779-1782) [**150**].[20]

One important consequence of the presence of Dutch traders overseas was the influx of hitherto unknown products to the United Provinces. Almost

---

18 "Physical description of an excellent collection of rare animals, consisting of East- and West-Indian quadrupeds, birds, and snakes."

19 "Treatise on the procreation and metamorphosis of the insects of Suriname."

20 "The exotic butterflies living in the three continents of Asia, Africa, and America."

FIG. 4.10 American animals, including a llama and a Mexican bull, from Simon de Vries, *Curieuse aenmerckingen der bysonderste Oost en West Indische verwonderens-waerdige dingen* (Utrecht, 1682).

During the first stages of their protracted war of independence, the Dutch primarily conceived of the New World as territories characterized as much by tyranny and bloodshed as Spanish rule in the Netherlands. Particularly Las Casas's account of the "destruction of the Indies" was grist to the mill of the revolt's ideologists. The Black Legend lost strength after peace was signed between Spain and the United Provinces, but never disappeared. Legends gave way to experience from the 1590s onward, as the Dutch ventured to the Americas themselves. In New Netherland, Brazil, and Suriname, they mapped the country and described the flora, fauna, and native inhabitants. In many ways, Dutch colonial scholarship still commands respect.

overnight, great interest arose in two indigenous American crops, tobacco and cacao. Both were, of course, in the first place luxury goods, but some ascribed healing properties to them. Tobacco was prescribed as a remedy for scurvy, gout, kidney stones, and gallstones. Cornelis Bontekoe (1647-1685), the Dutch court physician of King Frederick William of Prussia, was a zealous advocate of the virtues of chocolate. In his days, chocolate was almost exclusively consumed as a drink, which was prepared by mixing cocoa beans with vanilla, cinnamon, and sugar. Cocoa, Bontekoe wrote, contains more nutritious juice than meat and it does not have unpleasant side effects. It feeds all parts of the body, but mostly the brains; it satisfies one's thirst, and it protects against toothache, carbuncles, and inflammation. Other alleged advantages were that it would prevent narcolepsy and that it was a sovereign antidepressant.

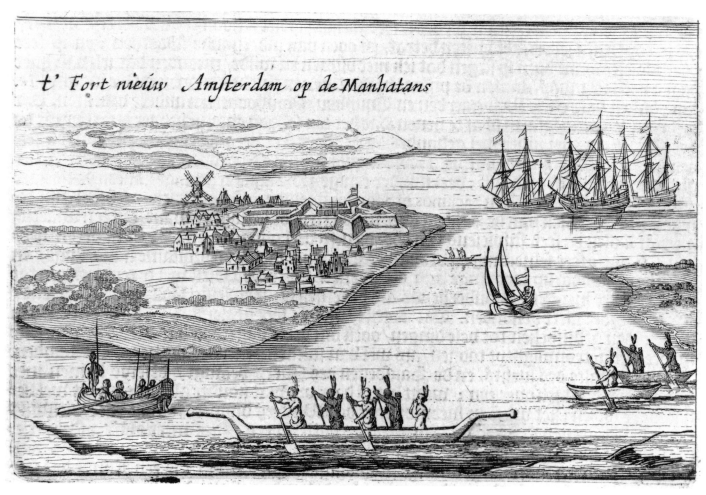

t' Fort nieuw Amsterdam op de Manhatans

FIG. 5.1 A rather inaccurate view of New Amsterdam in the first years after its foundation. It was probably based upon city plans not completely carried out. From *Beschrijvinghe van Virginia* (Amsterdam, 1651).

CHAPTER 5

"In Some Future Day It May Be Thought of More Importance": Dutch Contributions to North American History

The Dutch were not the only ones in the years around 1600 to search for a northeastern passage to the "spice islands." An explorer in the service of the English Muscovy Company, Henry Hudson (ca. 1565-1611), made a number of journeys, but never got beyond Novaya Zemlya. Despite these abortive attempts, Hudson persevered, even though investors in his home country were no longer willing to back him. Trying his luck in the Netherlands, Hudson met the famous "geo-theologian" Petrus Plancius. Earlier, Plancius had been among the organizers of the Dutch expeditions to find a northeastern route, all of which had failed. With Hudson, he now proposed an attempt to search to the north of Novaya Zemlya and obtained the support of the Dutch East India Company, although the Company directors were less than enthusiastic. On April 6, 1609, the yacht *Halve Maen* (Half Moon), of eighty tons, set sail from the Dutch island of Texel, with Hudson as captain.

The northern waters had an unpleasant surprise in store for the Anglo-Dutch crew: the planned route was full of ice. Hudson was forced to give in to the demands of his men who were suffering from the sharp cold and unwilling to continue. When Hudson suggested that the ship instead cross the Atlantic and search for a northwest passage the idea was well received. After a difficult voyage, Newfoundland was reached in July, and the search for a northwest passage began. Convinced of his eventual success, Hudson sailed southwest, trying every bay, inlet, and river mouth. Eventually, he ascended the broad river which since bears his name. The ensuing river journey, which took the *Halve Maen* as far as modern Albany, was marked by occasional encounters with natives looking for barter. The crewmen did not trust most Indians and killed some of them, although they struck up friendships with others. Lack of victuals finally obliged Hudson to return to Europe, with an astonishing achievement behind him for the benefit of the Dutch.

A short time later, Hudson once more sailed for North America, but this time in the service of the English again. This journey in 1611 proved to be his undoing. His crew mutinied in Hudson Bay and set him and his son adrift in a small boat. He was never seen again.

In the wake of Hudson, a number of Dutch merchants sailed to North America, encouraged by the good prospects for fur trading. Various firms entered into a fierce competition for otter and beaver skins, which were procured from the Indians in exchange for beads, knives, adzes, axes, and kettles. In 1614, these Dutch firms merged into a single

Albany

CONNECTICUT

Hudson R.

Connecticut R.

Delaware R.

N   E   T   H   E   R   L   A   N   D

N   E   W

Long Island Sound

New Amsterdam

Long Island

Susquehanna R.

NEW
SWEDEN

Nieuwer-
Amstel

Delaware Bay

Swanendael

A T L A N T I C

O C E A N

Chesapeake Bay

N

| 0 | | 50 km |
| 0 | | 50 mi |

MAP IV   North America

52

een Mahakuaes Indiaen, met hun Steden en woningen

FIG. 5.2 A Mahican Indian in front of two types of Indian villages, from *Beschrijvinghe van Virginia* (Amsterdam, 1651).

company, the New Netherland Company, which was granted the monopoly of sailing to "newly discovered lands situated in America between New France and Virginia, whereof the sea coasts lie between the 40th and 45th degrees of latitude, now named New Netherland."

The Dutch Colonization of North America

When the Dutch West India Company was founded in 1621 and set about colonizing, this whole area included only a few scattered trading posts. Among the first settlers of New Netherland were many Walloon families, who originated in the French-speaking parts of the southern Netherlands. In the summer of 1625 the construction of a fort was begun on Manhattan Island, and shortly afterwards the island itself was "bought" from the natives. It is unlikely, of course, that the Indians had the slightest notion of the European concept of property rights and realized the nature of this famous exchange. Absolute possession of land in perpetuity for exclusive use was not part of the vocabulary of northeastern woodland Indians.

The fort, called Amsterdam, was designed to protect the Dutch against their European enemies, Spain and England. This nucleus would develop into the town of New Amsterdam, which served as the seat of the Dutch government. The view that is included in Joost Hartgers' *Beschrijvinghe* [85][1] used to be considered the earliest printed view of New Amsterdam. It purports to show the colony in its infancy: the fort, some houses, a windmill, and a few ships. But this engraving is now generally regarded as a fantasy, or a representation based on plans that were never put into effect. (Fig. 5.1).

Because the costs of colonization exceeded the profits from the beaver trade, there was much discussion in the Dutch Republic on the question of whether a monopoly or free trade would be most advantageous for the state, anticipating a debate

1 *Beschrijvinghe van Virginia, Nieuw Nederlandt, Nieuw Engelandt, en d'eylanden Bermudes, Berbados, en S. Christoffel* ("Description of Virginia, New Netherland, New England, and the islands Bermuda, Barbados, and St. Christopher"). Amsterdam, 1651.

D' EEUWIGE GEDENCK - TEEKENĒ

vande Engelſe en Nederlandtſe Oorlog en VREEDE, geſloten tot Breda, op den 31 Iulij, en geratificeert op den 24 Auguſti, Anno 1667.

f.° 249

FIG. 5.3 Depicted here is the signing of the treaty in 1667 that ended the second Anglo-Dutch War. The event took place at Breda in the Netherlands. The treaty confirmed the Dutch possession of Suriname, which they had taken from the English that year, and the English possession of New York, taken from the Dutch in 1664. If there had been instead a return to the status quo ante bellum, the English would have regained Suriname and the Dutch recovered New York, with very different results in world history. The opinion of many at the time was that by securing Suriname, the Dutch got the better of the bargain, but the English were able to consolidate their territory along the Atlantic coast in a continuous string of possessions. From *Kort en bondigh verhael van 't geene in den oorlogh, tusschen den Koningh van Engelant &c. . . . der vrye Vereenigde Nederlanden* (Amsterdam, 1667).

about these same issues concerning the Dutch colony in Brazil. After the free trade supporters carried the day, an agreement was reached in 1629 on the method of private colonization. Outside of Manhattan Island, patroons, or manorial landowners, were to take up agriculture and stock-breeding. These exclusive few, who came from wealthy Dutch families, were granted huge territories in hereditary fief, provided that fifty colonists were settled there within three years' time to develop the territory. One patroonship suffered only a very short life: all thirty-two inhabitants of Swanendael, west of Delaware Bay, were killed by Indians less than a year after their arrival. The patroon, David Pietersz. de Vries, reported in his *Korte historiael* [**92**]² what he found when arriving a year after the massacre.

In general, relations between settlers and natives left much to be desired. Like other Europeans, Dutchmen expressed their surprise at the apparently unconstrained lives of the North American Indians, who were believed to live "sans roi, sans loi, sans foi." Because Indian religion seemed to lack a hierarchy, the Dutch assumed that Indian faith was hardly worthy of respect. The Minister Johannes Megapolensis argued in his *Een kort ontwerp van de Mahakvase Indianen*,³ a pamphlet included in Hartgers' *Beschrijvinghe* [**85**], that the Mohawks were complete strangers to religion, although they did esteem some sort of spirit in God's place and worshipped the Devil.

The Indians, for their part, as Adriaen van der Donck contended in *Beschryvinge van Nieuvv-Nederlant* (Amsterdam, 1655) [**91**],⁴ were amazed to see how little authority Megapolensis had over the conduct of his compatriots. The States General's advice to the first Dutch migrants, to convert the Indians to the true faith by good example as well as good instruction, was largely disregarded. The Indians concluded that the Christian religion could not be very high-principled considering how frequently the Christians misbehaved.

It was not just mutual incomprehension that plagued the relations between Native Americans and Europeans. Rash steps on the Dutch part also played a role, such as the decision to levy taxes on the Indians living in the vicinity of Manhattan. Although small-scale acts of vengeance from both sides left scars, peaceful coexistence prevailed on the whole until 1643. In that year, an armed Dutch expedition was dispatched against several groups of Indians that were on the run from the Mohawks and had sought refuge near New Amsterdam. On the initiative of governor Willem Kieft (1597-1647), many Indians were cruelly killed. In the decades to come, the Dutch would suffer the consequences of this massacre.

Tensions with the indigenous people were one of the problems in New Netherland. Others were the shortage of Dutch immigrants and the ground being lost in the entire northeast region to English settlers. Only one patroonship truly prospered: Rensselaerswijck, named after its proprietor Kiliaen van Rensselaer, a jewel merchant. In the first fifteen years after the start of colonization in 1624, a mere six hundred settlers had arrived in the vast region of New Netherland between the Delaware and Hudson Rivers. Moreover, this group included many foreign sojourners in the Netherlands who had emigrated to Holland from their native soil for economic or religious reasons. German Lutherans, English Puritans, East European Anabaptists, Mennonites, and Belgian Catholics were found in New Amsterdam in 1650, all of whom had come from Holland. While the Dutch Reformed doctrine had an official monopoly, private worship in other religious traditions was allowed, despite protests from local Dutch ministers.

In this respect, New Netherland was a copy of the Dutch Republic, where officials set great store by strict regard for freedom of conscience. The liberal climate of the United Provinces was one reason the English Pilgrims crossed the Channel in 1607 and 1608 to take up residence in Leiden. Estranged from England by the episcopal system and persecuted by the Archbishop of Canterbury, these "separatists" sought refuge in the Netherlands, where they arrived on the eve of the Twelve Years Truce. Their stay was never more than a temporary solution, since there was a world of difference between the Truce and a peace treaty. The threat of renewed warfare between the Netherlands and Spain was constantly on the horizon. Besides, the Pilgrim leaders feared assimilation into Dutch culture, and in the end opted for all the risks and hardship of the New World as a venue to carry out their ideals. Fate decreed that the Pilgrims sailed from England to America on board the *Mayflower* in the summer of 1620, although they very nearly embarked on a Dutch vessel bound for New Netherland.

---

2 *Korte historiael ende journaels aenteyckeninge van verscheyden voyagiens in de vier deelen des wereldts-ronde, als Europa, Africa, Asia, ende Amerika* ("Short history and notes of a journal of several voyages undertaken in the four parts of the globe, Europe, Africa, Asia, and America"). Hoorn and Alkmaar, 1655.

3 "Sketch of the Mohawk Indians."

4 "Description of New Netherland."

FIG. 5.4 The adventurous life of David de Vries included four trips to New Amsterdam in the ten years between 1633 and 1643, including one visit that extended into a five-year stay from 1638 to 1643. De Vries was involved with unsuccessful Dutch patroonships on Staten Island, on the Delaware River, and in Suriname, and he took part in negotiations with the Puritans in Connecticut over territorial claims between New England and New Netherland. His journals are a valuable primary source for the early history of New Amsterdam and include many observations on Indian life in the region. This portrait is from David Pietersz. de Vries, *Korte historiael ende journaels aenteyckeninge* (Hoorn and Alkmaar, 1655).

It is still unclear how settlers for New Netherland were eventually recruited. Most were probably encouraged to come by people already living in the colony, although some may have been persuaded by agents of patroons. It is doubtful that the printed promotional literature about America exerted any influence at all, even though there was no shortage of this literature. One of the tracts that has come down to us, typical of the genre, was the product of the pen of Jacob Steendam, a poet living in New Amsterdam. In *Klacht van Nieuw-Amsterdam* [95],[5] he sang the praises of the colony's milk, butter, and fruit. An anonymous booklet, *Kort verhael van Nieuw-Nederlants gelegentheit, deugden, natuerlijke voorrechten, en byzondere bequaemheidt ter bevolkingh* (1662) [99],[6] recommended the climate, and claimed that diseases were not found in New Netherland.

No man is so identified with the image of New Netherland as is Pieter Stuyvesant (1611-1672). He had served the West India Company in various capacities in Brazil and in 1643 was appointed governor of Curaçao. Badly injured during a Dutch attack on what was then the Spanish island of St. Martin, he started out as New Netherland's governor in 1647 with a wooden leg. For the Dutch in North America, Stuyvesant's position and reputation may be compared with the prominence of Johan Maurits in Brazil. Both men were great personalities, strong leader types, tenacious by nature, and excellent representatives of their country. But while Johan Maurits preached religious tolerance, Stuyvesant had little use for anyone who was not a Dutch Calvinist. His hostile and insolent behavior towards Jews and Quakers found no favor in the sight of the Board of Nineteen back home.

Stuyvesant's predecessors would have been unable to cope with the manifold problems he had to face during his government. Continuous cross-border conflicts with the English and Swedes took up much of his time and tried his patience, although the Dutch found a peaceful solution to their problems with English colonists by conceding the Connecticut Valley and most of Long Island. In Delaware, the pursuit of Dutch fur-trading interests was impeded by the colony of New Sweden. While

5 *Klacht van Nieuw-Amsterdam, in Nieuw-Nederlandt, tot haar moeder: van haar begin, wasdom en tegenwoordigen stand* ("Complaint made by New Amsterdam in New Netherland to her mother about her start, growth and present state"). Amsterdam, 1659.
6 "Short account of New Netherland's situation, virtues, natural privileges, and singular fitness for population."

Dutch interests in the area had suffered from neglect under Governor Kieft, Stuyvesant took a more energetic approach. Stuyvesant perceived New Sweden in Delaware as a threat, since settlers there were believed to be living within the boundaries of New Netherland, and the Swedes had prevented the Dutch from establishing a settlement on the Schuylkill River. Having first led a successful military expedition that dismantled the old Dutch Fort Nassau and relocated it on the west side of the Delaware River, Stuyvesant simply conquered New Sweden in 1655.

The Dutch colony that was planted on the spot was off to a bad start. In general, Nieuwer-Amstel, on the site of present-day New Castle, was too much a drain on the WIC budget. Impoverished by the failure of New Holland (Dutch Brazil), in 1656 the Company ceded the Delaware colony to the city of Amsterdam, which immediately started sending soldiers and recruiting settlers.

English Rule and English Culture

And then, suddenly, it was all over. In August 1664 New Netherland ceased to exist after a squadron of four English ships appeared off the coast of New Amsterdam with a substantial fleet, catching the colonial authorities by surprise. Stuyvesant was quite alone in his desire to resist the intruders and surrendered reluctantly before York's superior strength. The showdown occurred without a drop of blood being shed, in part because the English promised not to interfere with Dutch Reformed practice and to protect Dutch trade.

In 1673-74 the Dutch were briefly able once more to seize control of New York. Their reconquest was followed by the introduction of a set of measures intended to establish a strict religious order. Keeping of the Sabbath was enforced, and bans were imposed on dancing, playing cards, and picking strawberries on Sundays. English rule, however, was soon restored, and the way was cleared for the gradual Anglicization of the Dutch population. Being part of the colonial elite in the community, the well-to-do Dutch merchants adapted most easily to the changed circumstances. But for a substantial number of Dutchmen, especially the religious pietists, Anglicization in general proceeded far from quietly.

When news of the Glorious Revolution in England reached New York in 1689, with the accession to the English throne of the Dutch stadholder William of Orange, a full-scale rebellion broke out in New York City. Led by a German-born merchant and militia captain, Jacob Leisler, the rebellion split the Dutch community, with Leisler receiving his greatest support from the more pietistic Protestants. In the end, however, after less than two years, Leisler's rebellion was suppressed, and he himself executed.

In the following decades, the Dutch share of New York's population declined steadily. By the early eighteenth century, the English outnumbered the Netherlanders for the first time. Immigration from the United Provinces had reached a nadir, while Leisler's defeat induced many inhabitants to move up the Hudson river or to start a new life in New Jersey. But the Dutch did not spread out much further, so that by 1790 eighty percent of the 100,000 persons of Dutch ancestry in the United States were still living within a 150-mile radius of New York City. In King's County (Brooklyn) and up-river, the Dutch were a major political and social force, and they continued to be a potent influence in Manhattan and on Staten Island.

The persistence of Dutch culture is evidenced by the printing press. Although there was no Dutch printing in New Netherland while the Dutch were in control of the colony, by the 1730s, John Peter Zenger and other English-language printers were issuing works in Dutch, such as Cornelius van Santvoord's *Samenspraak over de Klaghte der Raritanders* (New York, 1726) [135],[7] primarily to meet the demand for religious books and pamphlets. Some 100 titles in the Dutch language appeared in the eighteenth century, although for half of these no extant copies have survived. Even for the extant titles, the surviving copies are so few that these Dutch imprints are among the rarest of the rare in early American books.

Although a certain Dutchness was preserved in religion, conceptions of land distribution, and family relations, the Dutch language was increasingly threatened since the middle of the eighteenth century. Ministers sent by the Classis of Amsterdam found it difficult to make themselves understood in the Middle Colonies. The English language soon took hold in Dutch churches, and in 1772 the subordination of the English-speaking Dutch Reformed Church in America to the classis of the Dutch-speaking Reformed Church of the Netherlands was ended.

---

7 "Dialogue concerning the complaint of the people from Raritan."

Dutch Support for the Revolution

The revolution for independence in the 1770s and 1780s found both Dutch ministers and laymen divided along regional and religious lines. Some Dutch Americans played an active role in the fight for independence. One of them was Pierre van Cortlandt. He was appointed chairman of the Committee of Safety of the Colony of New York and in January 1776 edited *To the inhabitants of the colony of New-York* [**146**], a collection of documents dealing with the war between the Thirteen Colonies and the mother country.

Other Revolutionaries were actually born in the United Provinces, such as Bernard Romans (ca. 1720-1784), who moved to England as a youth, and went to North America as an adult. He fought on the battlefields of the war for independence, but also served the patriot cause with his pen, holding up the Dutch resistance to Spain as an example to the North Americans in his two-volume *Annals of the troubles in the Netherlands* (Hartford, 1778-1782) [**147**]. He advertised this work by saying it had been written "to evince the great hardships and amazing success of a vassal people who extricated themselves from the tyranny of the most exorbitant power of Europe [Spain], and in the end ruined that power while the ocean was covered with its navy, and the earth with its armies."

The Founding Fathers, indeed, pored over the Dutch example of successful national resistance two hundred years earlier, which explains the many similarities between the Declaration of Independence and the *Plakkaat van Verlatinge*, which had served as the Dutch renunciation of Habsburg authority in the sixteenth century. In the Netherlands of the late eighteenth century, however, the Founding Fathers were looking for more than just inspiration. In the course of the Revolutionary War, France had lent the newly independent United States large sums of money, but additional loans were needed. In 1780, John Adams was sent to the Netherlands for this purpose. In order to increase his chances of obtaining loans, Adams deemed it necessary to gain diplomatic recognition of his country by the Dutch Republic. He mounted a public relations campaign, drawing up two lengthy memorandums, one for the stadholder and one for the States General, and arranging for a collection of newspaper articles of his own, originally published in the *Boston Gazette* in 1775, to appear in Dutch: *Geschiedenis van het geschil* (Amsterdam, 1782) [**154**].[8] This book even includes engravings of Adams by the Dutch artist Reinier Vinkeles. One of the memorandums Adams sent to the States General was printed in *A collection of state-papers*.[9] His message was that "the originals of the two Republics are so much alike, that a history of one seems but a transcript from that of the other: so that every Dutchman instructed in the subject, must pronounce the American revolution just and necessary, or pass a censure upon the greatest actions of his immortal ancestors." Other historic ties between the United States and the Netherlands recalled by Adams included the Pilgrim Fathers, New Netherland, and the similarity of Calvinist public religion and clerical discipline.

In the Netherlands, Adams befriended a man in Leiden named François Adriaan van der Kemp (1752-1829). In times of revolutionary upheaval, this Mennonite preacher was like a fish in water. In the politically strife-torn Netherlands of the 1780s, where supporters of the stadholder faced the Patriot movement, which propagated ideas foreshadowing the French Revolution, Van der Kemp affiliated with the latter. He joined a Patriot volunteer militia company, only to be taken prisoner by the Prince of Orange's troops in 1787. After having escaped to America in 1788, he spent most of the rest of his life in northern New York state.

It was at Adams's instigation that in 1781 Van der Kemp edited the propagandist collection *Verzameling van stukken tot de dertien Vereenigde Staeten van Noord-America betrekkelijk* (Leiden, 1781) [**152**],[10] a compilation of documents designed to influence Dutch public opinion. It included, among other items, the Articles of Confederation, an address by John Hancock, and a speech in which a preference was expressed for U.S. society over life in the Netherlands. In the United Provinces, Roman Catholics were said to be second-class citizens, whereas full equality had been reached in the land of Washington and Jefferson.

On April 19, 1782, the Dutch acknowledged Adams's status as an official U.S. envoy, which meant that for practical purposes they recognized the United States as an independent country. The anonymous poem *Lierzang op de verklaarde onafhanglijkheid der Noord-Amerikaansche Staaten*

---

8 "History of the dispute."

9 An American, *A collection of state-papers, relative to the first acknowledgment of the sovereignty of the United States of America, and the reception of their Minister Plenipotentiary, by their High Mightinesses the States General of the United Netherlands*. London, 1782.

10 "Collection of papers regarding the United States of North America."

(Dordrecht, 1782) [**153**][11] celebrated this break-through. Its message was clear and full of enlight-ened self-interest: friendship with the North Americans would pay off, for it would revive Dutch trade, which was going through a severe crisis.

In July, Adams secured a $2 million loan by arrangements with three Amsterdam banking houses. For the next two years, this loan was the main finan-cial resource for the U.S. treasury, virtually saving the fledgling country from bankruptcy. Decades later, in 1823, Adams wrote to Van der Kemp about his expe-rience with the Dutch:

> I modestly blush for my nation when I consider the sangfroid, the nonchalance, with which they have received the magnifical testimonies of the esteem, confidence and affection of the Dutch towards the United States, and the low estimation in which we have held the importance of their connections with us. Their separation from England, union with France and Spain and their treaty with us was the event which ultimately turned the scale of the American Revolutionary war and produced the peace of 1783. But the truth is that neither France nor England nor the friends of France or England in America would even acknowledge it to be of any weight and con-sequently it has fallen into total oblivion. But in some future day it may be thought of more importance.[12]

---

11 "Lyrical poem on the declared independence of the North American states."

12 Quoted in J.W. Schulte Nordholt, *The Dutch Republic and American Independence* (Chapel Hill and London, 1982).

FIG. 6.1 The colonial headquarters in Berbice, a Dutch colony from
1627 until 1796, from Jan Jacob Hartsinck, *Beschryving van Guiana, of
de wildekust in Zuid-America* (Amsterdam, 1770).

CHAPTER 6

The Guianas and the Caribbean Islands

The Dutch presence in Guiana dates back to the mid-1590s, when a trading post was established some twenty miles up the Amazon, and another one seven miles further. A fort built in 1596 at the point where the Cuyuni and Mazaruni Rivers join the Essequibo was destroyed by the Spaniards after less than a year. Nevertheless, Dutch explorers went up the Amazon further and further, on the way acquainting themselves with tobacco, a New World crop they soon started to cultivate. Also, a modest barter trade was organized with neighboring Indian villages. In general, exploration and colonization of this so-called "Wild Coast" was predominantly carried out by Zeelanders with some help from Englishmen.

Dutch Ventures on the Wild Coast

The main public agency promoting the founding of settlements in the New World at the turn of the century was the States of Holland, which in 1614 passed a resolution encouraging settlement in the Americas and offering a trade monopoly for some years to pioneers. The results, however, were meager. After the West India Company took over control of Dutch activities in the Atlantic, immigration to Guiana was no more satisfactory than it was to New Netherland. The main reason migration failed was that trade fell short of expectations. Travelling through Guiana in this period, David Pietersz. de Vries, one of the patroons of New Netherland, observed that dyewood was the only interesting trade item [**92**]. In 1633, a WIC report described the level of native civilization in the Guianas in no uncertain terms: "These nations are barbarous and have few needs; they do not dress nor do the people need to work for their support; hence all trade that is possible there can be handled by two or three ships annually and sustained by little capital."

Although settlements in the Guianas remained few and small, the Dutch presence was deemed sufficiently permanent at the peace negotiations in Munster in 1648 to lead Spain to cede Essequibo and Berbice. The arrival in these small colonies in 1654 of groups of Dutchmen from New Holland (following the reconquest of Dutch Brazil by the Portuguese) prompted the Company once more to promote colonization in the region. Lacking funds of its own, the administration of the first two settlements devolved to the Zeeland towns of Middelburg, Veere, and Flushing. Essequibo was later entrusted to the Zeeland Chamber of the WIC. In Cayenne, the Chamber of Amsterdam assumed responsibility for a colony that had been started by a patroon who was pressed for money. The Chamber tried to attract

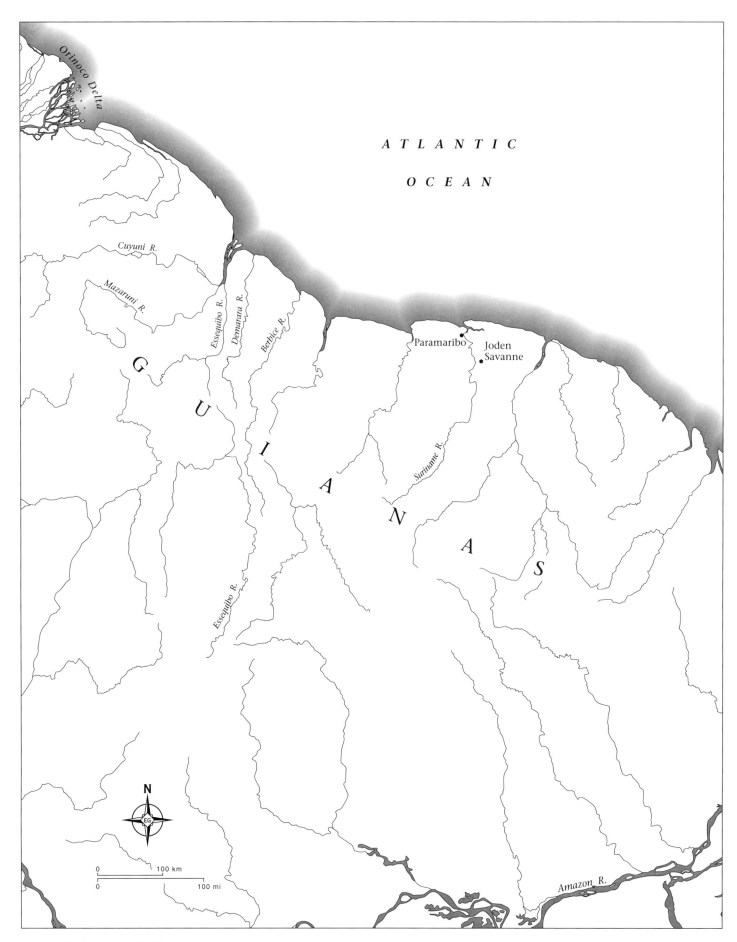

MAP IV   Suriname and the Guianas

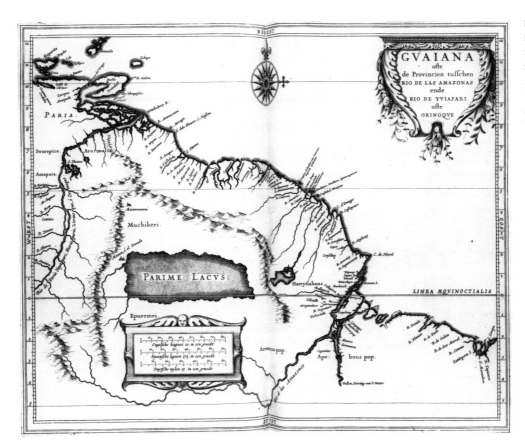

FIG. 6.2 Guiana, an area first settled by the Dutch in the 1590s. This map from Joannes de Laet, *Nieuvve wereldt* (Leiden, 1625) shows El Dorado and the imaginary "Parime Lacus."

settlers by promising ten years of tax freedom and postponement of payment for slaves, but in 1663, the French conquered Cayenne, bringing Dutch activity there to an abrupt end.

The other Guiana colonies remained barren places, despite the absurd assurance in one promotional tract that this area could produce seven annual harvests. The author, a former captain in Dutch Brazil, argued that once poor people had arrived in Guiana and sat down to have a meal, they would think "they were having a banquet with Anthony at the table of Cleopatra" [**94**].[1] An allegation in another book, interestingly, combined the Black Legend with the myth of El Dorado. It pointed out that the interior of South America, the hinterland of the Wild Coast, still contained hidden treasures; Spanish tyranny, however, by alienating the Indians had kept the conquerors from the secret. Settlement plans continued to be made, not only for Guiana proper, but also for the Amazon region. Johannes Reeps, a merchant from Hoorn, received a patent in 1689, for example, for a colony on the west bank of the Amazon River [**121**].[2] Eventually, Reeps sailed from Flushing, but his ship foundered on the coast of Brazil. Although he made his way in a sloop with seventeen passengers to Dutch-held Suriname by way of Belém and Cayenne, the colony was never founded.

The late seventeenth century did see the beginning of the development of Essequibo. Barter with the Indians from trading posts that were increasingly penetrating the interior proved to be lucrative. In the eighteenth century, plantation agriculture superseded commerce, although the utilization of mangrove swamps in the coastal plains required irrigation and drainage, and therefore a large capital outlay. The key figure in Essequibo's transformation was Laurens Storm van 's Gravesande. As the colony's ruler for thirty consecutive years, between 1742 and 1772, his major accomplishment was the establishment of friendly relations with inland Indians, who had hitherto been captured and enslaved.

---

1 O.K. [Otto Keye], *Het waere onderscheydt tusschen koude en warme landen* ("The true difference between cold and warm lands"). The Hague, 1659.

2 *Copia van 't octroy door de Hoogh Mog. Heeren Staten Generael der Vereenigde Nederlanden, gegeven aan Jan Reeps, en syne mede participanten* ("Copy of the patent issued by the High and Mighty States General of the United Netherlands, issued to Jan Reeps and his fellow participants"). The Hague, 1689.

FIG. 6.3 "The curious way in which an Indian is initiated as a captain." From Adriaan van Berkel, *Amerikaansche voyagien, behelzende een reis na Rio de Berbice* (Amsterdam, 1695).

een Wonderlyke Manier hoe een Indiaan tot Capityn gemaakt werd.

Storm took the step of inviting English planters in the Caribbean to settle in Essequibo, as well as in Demerara, where he also held sway. The colony, however, did not lose its Dutch appearance, as a British visitor noted in 1796: "I could have fancied myself in Holland. The land appeared as one wide flat intersected with dykes and canals—the roads mere banks of mud and clay, thrown from the ditches at their sides—and the houses bedaubed and painted in tawdry colors, like Dutch toys, giving the whole a striking resemblance to the mother country" [**168**].[3]

The author of these lines was George Pinckard, a medical doctor who accompanied the British troops at their invasion of Demerara in 1796. Late in the eighteenth century, the settlements in the Guianas changed hands with extraordinary frequency. They fell under British control in 1781, became French a year afterwards, Dutch again in 1784, only to be occupied again by Great Britain.

Berbice had been a Dutch settlement since the Flushing merchant and West India Company director Abraham van Pere in 1627 had agreed to found a patroonship there. In 1720, the Society of Berbice took over from the Van Pere family. Under the lead of this joint-stock company, the colony experienced rapid growth. While Adriaan van Berkel had counted five plantations in the late seventeenth century [**124**],[4] eight more plantations, maintaining some one hundred slaves each, had been added by 1722.

The remarkable change the colony was undergoing was observed in several contemporary works [**134**].[5] In the second half of the eighteenth century, a huge capital inflow had even more profound economic consequences. Sugar production was diminished in favor of coffee, and new plantations shifted the center of production from the interior back to the coast.

This process was well under way when a tenacious epidemic in the early 1760s, probably dysentery, decimated the white population. Soldiers, craftsmen, and clerks serving the Society of Berbice died by the dozens. A large group of slaves, who had been the victims for many years of beastly treatment by their masters, seized upon this opportunity to kill many whites. Everything went off well for the blacks at first, who almost drove their opponents into the sea in their attempt to take over the colony, but at that crucial

---

3 *Notes on the West Indies: written during the expedition under the command of the late General Sir Ralph Abercromby.* London, 1806.

4 *Amerikaansche voyagien, behelzende een reis na rio de Berbice, gelegen op het vaste land van Guiana, aan de wilde-kust van America* ("American voyages, including a trip to Rio de Berbice, located on the mainland of Guyana, on the Wild Coast of America"). Amsterdam, 1695.

5 *Beschryving van de rivier en colonie der Barbice, geleegen aan de wilde kust van Gujana, bewesten van Suriname* ("Description of the river and colony of Berbice, located on the Wild Coast of Guyana, West of Suriname"). Amsterdam, 1725.

FIG. 6.4 Ritual burning of offerings and belongings of the deceased at a Native American funeral in Berbice. From *Kortbondige beschryvinge van de colonie de Berbice* (Amsterdam, 1763).

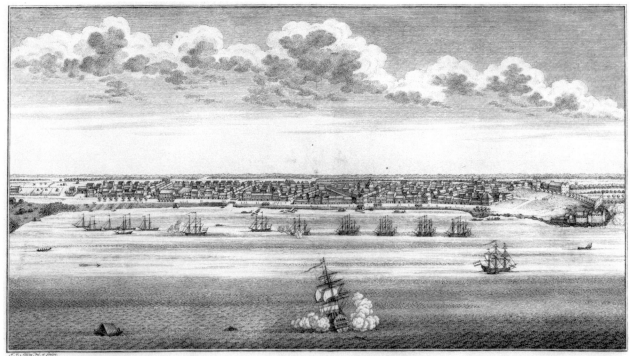

GEZICHT VAN DE STAD PARAMARIBO EN HET FORT ZELANDIA IN SURINAME.

FIG. 6.5 The Dutch headquarters in Suriname with the city of Paramaribo, from Jan Jacob Hartsinck, *Beschryving van Guiana, of de Wilde Kust in Zuid-America* (Amsterdam, 1770).

point difficulties arose. Internal dissension among them about military strategy was rife and a fundamental omission was beginning to make itself felt: the slaves had failed to set up an adequate food supply.

It was bow or break for the whites, who found themselves confined to a small strip of land in late March, 1763. But new troops were called in from St. Eustatius and Suriname, and Berbice was ultimately reconquered. Scores were settled with the rebels in a harsh way. Eighteen months had elapsed from the start of the rebellion in February 1763 to the last executions, and when the smoke cleared, the colony had lost almost half of its black and perhaps an even larger percentage of its white population. The rebellion came just too late to be discussed in a 1763 narrative *Kortbondige beschryvinge van de colonie de Berbice* [**141**],[6] but the events received ample treatment in Jan Jacob Hartsinck's *Beschryving van Guiana, of de wildekust, in Zuid-America* (Amsterdam, 1770) [**143**].[7] Evidently biased against the blacks, Hartsinck asserted, in contrast with the slaves' own testimonies, that the slaves had not been customarily treated in a brutal way at all.

Although the rebellion had shocked the white elite and revealed the hazards of the system, slavery continued to be the economic foundation of the colony. Decades later, George Pinckard [**168**] found a slave auction to be an important social event in New Amsterdam, as the colonial capital of Berbice came to be called: "On arriving at the town, we were surprized to find it quite a holiday, or a kind of public fair. The sale seemed to have excited general attention, and to have brought together all the inhabitants of the colony. The planters came down from the estates with their wives and families all arrayed in their gayest apparel: the belles and beaux appeared in their Sunday suits: even the children were in full-dress; and their slaves decked out in holiday clothes. It was quite a gala-day, and greater numbers of people were collected than we had supposed to have been in the colony."

The Plantation Colony of Suriname

In 1667, during the second Anglo-Dutch war, the States of Zeeland sent a squadron of seven ships including three frigates to the Wild Coast to take revenge on the English for the havoc caused there in the last war. A surprise attack by a Dutch force of a

---

6 "Concise description of the colony of Berbice."
7 "Description of Guiana, or the Wild Coast, in South-America."

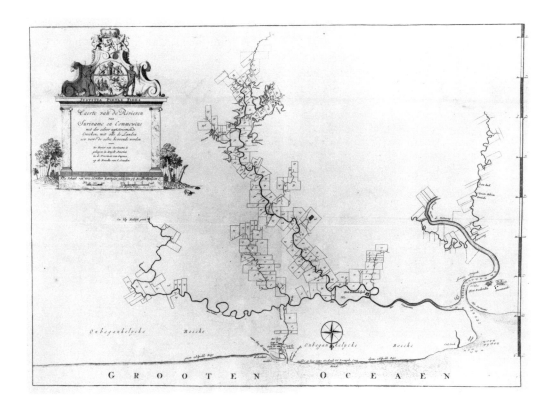

FIG. 6.6 Frederik de Wit, *Caerte van de rivieren van Suriname en Commowine met der selver uyt-stroomende creecken* (Amsterdam, 1688). Twenty years after the Dutch takeover of Suriname, many plantations had been laid out along the Cottica, Commewijne, and Suriname Rivers.

thousand men, led by Abraham Crijnssen, resulted in their conquest of Suriname. An English colony since 1651, Suriname had been the patroonship of Francis Willoughby. Along with the Willoughbys, many English planters packed their bags, leaving Suriname with only 280 men and women in a country about four times the size of the Netherlands.

The Dutch colony was initially ruled by the States of Zeeland, but financial problems induced them to sell it off to the West India Company, which itself was lacking in funds. Administration was eventually entrusted to the Society of Suriname, in which the WIC, the city of Amsterdam, and the nobleman Cornelis van Aerssen van Sommelsdijck (1637-1688) all participated evenly. Van Aerssen was appointed governor, but he proved to be an incompetent manager. The haughty attitude he assumed gave rise to disputes with planters and other settlers, eventually leading to his assassination by mutinous cavalrymen. Even so, the Sommelsdijck family continued to invest in Suriname for almost a century.

As in the case of previous Dutch ventures in the New World, settling the colony with Europeans proved to be a major problem in Suriname. Even scoundrels from the bridewells were sent to work as servants and laborers. On the other hand, the official religious tol-erance had a magnetic attraction for people of various denominations. The lepidoptrist and artist Maria Sibylla Merian, for instance, earlier mentioned, was an adherent of the Labadists. She had left her husband in Germany and moved to the Netherlands to join a colony founded by this pietist sect. In the process she underwent a total spiritual transformation that must have reminded her of the development of the butter-fly, an insect that she had studied extensively. At a cas-tle owned by the Sommelsdijck family in the vicinity of the Labadists' community, she saw preserved butter-flies from Suriname, an encounter that led her to trav-el to the Caribbean colony where she lived for two years, occupying herself as a painter of caterpillers and butterflies.

Most conspicuous of those who came to avoid per-secution were the Jews and French Huguenots. Sephardic and German Jews settled in the Joden Savanne (the Jewish Savannah), where a synagogue was erected in 1685 [**160**].[8] Protected by the Dutch

---

8 *Essai historique sur la colonie de Surinam, sa fondation, ses révo-lutions. . . . Avec l'histoire de la nation juive portugaise & alle-mande y établie* ("Historical essay on the colony of Suriname, its foundation, its revolutions. Including the history of the Portuguese and German Jewish nation established there"). Paramaribo, 1788.

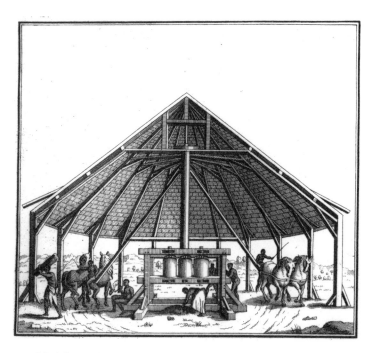

FIG. 6.7 A horse-driven sugar mill in Suriname, from Philippe Fermin, *Nieuwe algemeene beschryving van de colonie van Suriname* (Harlingen, 1770).

authorities, the Jews nevertheless even in Suriname faced increasingly overt manifestations of anti-semitism as the eighteenth century wore on. This tendency found expression, for example, in a regulation that excluded Jews from access to the colony's theater.

The most notable characteristic of the Suriname Jews was their dedication to agriculture. The colony grew into the largest Jewish agrarian settlement in the world. The relatively tolerant climate must have played a major role in this development, as well as the encouragement of plantation agriculture by the authorities. The Society of Suriname had set its mind on creating a "second Brazil" on the Wild Coast. In due course, Suriname would blossom into an important plantation colony producing sugar, coffee, cocoa, and cotton, even though the conditions under which this was accomplished were hardly ideal. Among other problems, the coastal strip where many plantations were located was flooded time and again by high tides. The planters succeeded, nevertheless, in making Suriname the colony with the highest productivity in the Americas. Massive drainage and irrigation helped to increase the number of plantations from 100 to 400 in the course of the eighteenth century. By the time the farming expert Anthony Blom published his book on the plantation economy after a twenty-year stay in Suriname [**158**],[9] there were fifty thousand slaves at work.

Lacking cultural homogeneity, Suriname contrasted markedly with the societies of Spanish America, where the Roman Catholic Church was the binding factor. The authority of Suriname's Protestant church was weak, and planters preferred playing ball on Sundays to dressing up for church. What is more, it was forbidden to introduce slaves to Christianity, out of fear that the teaching would encourage rebellion.

For a long time, the power of the planters was almost unlimited. The WIC, to be sure, appointed the governor, but this official had to cooperate with a Council whose candidates were nominated by the colonists. The wealthy planters, therefore, often were the dominant voice in matters of importance. Still, not all were interested in local politics, being eager only to return to the Netherlands as soon as they had accumulated a small fortune. This *animus revertendi*—as one of the colony's governors called it—left its imprint on the colony.

In the eighteenth century, the planters were tied increasingly to mortgage-granting merchant-bankers in the Netherlands. The lack of investment opportunities in the mother country had created a surplus of capital for which Suriname provided an outlet, all the more since coffee prices were constantly rising on the world market. The acquisition of bonds by metropolitan investors rendered money available for loans to planters. Plantation real estate valuations, however, were often groundless, so that these loans bore little relation to the actual value of the properties. When the moment came to settle their debts, the planters were often not able to pay, and many plantations ended up in the hands of metropolitan creditors.

Most planters settled down in the capital city of the colony to escape the lonely life of the interior and to be safe from attacks by runaway slaves, who often hid in the woods close to the plantations. Suriname was reputed to have a particularly harsh planter regime, but it was probably not very different from other plantation colonies in the Americas, all of which produced human misery as well as commodities. The slaves were allowed to work for themselves on Sundays and to use the income this labor produced to fulfill their own needs. According to Herlein, the money or barter was used to buy tobacco, *dram* (Surinamese rum), and fancy bands to wear around the waist [**130**].[10]

9 *Verhandeling van den landbouw in de colonie Suriname* ("Treatise on agriculture in the colony of Suriname"). Amsterdam, 1787.

10 *Beschryvinge van de volk-plantinge Zuriname* ("Description of the colony of Suriname"). Leeuwarden, 1718.

FIG. 6.8 Surinamese planters
used a tent-boat for transport
to the city of Paramaribo. From
Philippe Fermin, *Nieuwe algemeene beschryving van de colonie
van Suriname* (Harlingen, 1770).

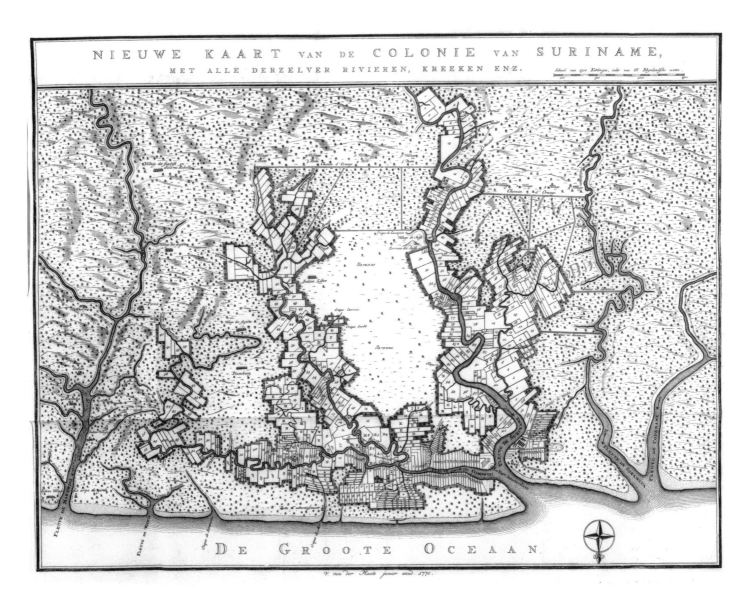

FIG. 6.9 The plantations of Suriname at the time of the loans crash.
From Philippe Fermin, *Nieuwe algemeene beschryving van de colonie van
Suriname* (Harlingen, 1770).

FIG. 6.10 A "Touvinga," a Surinamese black with only two fingers and two toes, from Jan Jacob Hartsinck, *Beschryving van Guiana, of de Wilde Kust, in Zuid-America* (Amsterdam, 1770).

Although Africans maintained a large majority over whites (sixty-five to one in the rural areas), as did recently-arrived blacks over seasoned slaves, they were subjected to heavy labor and endured harsh treatment. Consequently, ever-swelling numbers of slaves escaped. These maroons received considerable treatment in a book by the physician Philippe Fermin, who spent eight years in the colony [**144**].[11] Mostly deserting individually or in small groups, blacks in some instances joined to form substantial and permanent maroon communities. Inevitably, these slave outposts provoked an armed response from the colonial authorities, but military measures failed to have the intended effect, since the white soldiers lacked experience in jungle warfare and many of them fell early prey to tropical diseases. Eventually, various maroon settlements were tacitly accepted and recognized by the whites, but new maroon groups sprang up continuously, and the wars with the Dutch extended well into the nineteenth century.

The horrific wars are described in much detail in a work that has gone through more than twenty-five editions in six languages, making it the best-known book on eighteenth-century Suriname: John Gabriel Stedman's *Narrative, of a five years' expedition, against the revolted negroes of Surinam, in Guiana, on the Wild Coast of South America* (London, 1796) [**164**]. In the original manuscript, the Scotsman Stedman had denounced the degrading treatment of slaves which he had witnessed during his stay as a captain in the troops that fought the maroons. Yet, Stedman's contemporary editor mutilated his text to the effect that the author's actual views were obscured. Only in the twentieth century has an unexpurgated version of Stedman been published.

The John Carter Brown Library possesses a number of detailed maps from the early days of the Dutch era in Suriname. The situation at the time of their invasion is shown clearly on a map by John Thornton, *A new draught of Surranam upon the coast of Guianna* (London, ca. 1675) [**110**], based on an unknown English manuscript map. Another manuscript map, *A Discription of the Coleny of Surranam in Guiana Drawne in the Yeare 1667* [**104**], was probably drawn with an eye to the negotiations in Breda. The first map from the Dutch period was made by Frederik de Wit [**120**]. Plantations are indicated, but without the names of the planters.

One of the gems of the Library's collection of maps is that of Alexander de Lavaux, *Algemeene kaart van de colonie of provintie van Suriname* [**140**], which contains a wealth of information on Surinamese society and indicates the location of both plantations and maroon communities. This map, produced after 1758, is an updated version of a map that Lavaux had brought out twenty years before. As a young ensign of German descent, Lavaux had entered the service of the Society of Suriname in 1729. The campaigns against the maroons took him directly inland, where he immediately started to draw maps. In due course, he was enabled to have his general map of Suriname engraved in copperplate.

The Caribbean Islands

Halfway through the seventeenth century, Dutch activities in the Caribbean entered a new phase. Hitherto, the Dutch presence had been mostly characterized by privateering, but this activity was progressively replaced by trade, especially after the peace treaty of Munster in 1648. The Dutch carrying trade was in fact vital to the development of the

---

11 *Nieuwe algemeene beschryving van de colonie van Suriname* ("New general description of the colony of Suriname"). Harlingen, 1770.

FIG. 6.11 In 1668, four hundred buccaneers, led by Henry Morgan, captured the Spanish fort of Porto Bello near Panama. From Alexandre Olivier Exquemelin, *De Americaensche zee-roovers* (Amsterdam, 1678).

French and some English islands. The Dutch also played a key role in the introduction of the sugar industry to these colonies. During the English Civil War, between 1642 and 1649, the imports and exports of Barbados were in Dutch hands, and large amounts of tropical crops reached the ports of the Netherlands. Likewise, for at least two decades, the 1640s and 1650s, the supremacy of Dutch trade in the French West Indies was uncontested, and French historiography still credits the Dutch today for having helped Guadeloupe and Martinique through the difficult early plantation years. Eventually, however, the mercantilist measures adopted by the imperial powers forced the Dutch out of the French and English islands in the Caribbean.

The Dutch also tried to develop their own island colonies in the region. From 1628 there was a Zeeland settlement on Tobago. Sixty-eight colonists were the vanguard of a stream of Dutchmen, including both free settlers and indentured servants, who tried their luck on the island over a period of fifty years, defying both Spanish and Indian hostility as well as the claims of the Baltic Duke of Courland. In 1678, however, a French force conquered Tobago, and Dutch aspirations were buried.

Shortly after the Zeelanders had installed themselves on Tobago, the flag of the West India Company was raised over three small islands off the Venezuelan coast: Aruba, Bonaire, and Curaçao, and at the same time the Windward Islands of St. Eustatius, St. Maarten, and Saba were occupied as well. The salt pans were the main asset of St. Maarten, but little profit was to be made from them before the Peace of Munster, which formally assigned part of the island to the United Provinces. The other part of St. Maarten was and still is French. St. Eustatius' tobacco cultivation at first showed great promise, but the proceeds turned out to be disappointing. Given its limited natural resources, it was no major disaster that England and France occupied "Statia" for many years before it was returned to the Dutch in 1681.

Aruba and Bonaire were predestined to be a horse ranch and a salt pan, respectively. They were not in the same league as Curaçao, which developed with remarkable speed into an entrepôt. Curaçao had been conquered by the Dutch during the Eighty Years War for its value as a strategic naval base off the Spanish American mainland, from which raids into enemy territory could be easily organized. But once peace arrived in 1648, Curaçao was a liability rather than an asset, since the poor soil did not allow for large-scale cultivation of tropical crops. The

FIG. 6.12 The man in the middle is probably Jan Erasmus Reining, ordering his men to catch manatees and turtles. From Dionysius van der Sterre, *Zeer aanmerkelijke reysen gedaan door Jan Erasmus Reining* (Amsterdam, 1691).

Company directors even flirted with the idea of abandoning the three Leeward Islands, which had not yielded any material gain, but stopped short of implementing this plan. After 1660, however, Curaçao finally came into its own as an entrepôt where regional supply and demand could be harmonized. An increasing number of traders there specialized in the purchase of crops produced at different foreign colonies in the region and the exchange of these for European products filtered through Amsterdam and Zeeland.

The considerable value of the goods exchanged made Curaçao an attractive target for privateers and warfaring nations, yet the island never came under a foreign flag in the days of the WIC. An account of a failed French attack in 1673 is given in *Omstandigh verhael van de Fransche rodomontade voor het Fort Curassao* (1673) [**107**].[12] At least 1,200 Frenchmen had gathered to storm the fort where the Dutch had entrenched themselves, but in the end they lacked the courage to proceed.

Even the buccaneer fraternity, consisting of hundreds of pirates, never captured the fort, although they were a fearsome opponent of any colonial settlement they happened to select for their forays. The still classic account of the lives of the buccaneers flowed out of the pen of a man who lived in their midst for many years. The French physician Alexandre Olivier Exquemelin had done his medical exams in Amsterdam before he sailed for the Caribbean. His famous book, *De Americaensche zee-roovers* [**113**],[13] was first published in Dutch and went through many editions in French, English, Spanish, and German. By 1700, it had become an international best-seller.

The motley crowd of buccaneers included Jan Erasmus Reining from Zeeland. His three-year stay on Hispaniola and his Caribbean adventures were chronicled by another physician, the Curaçaoan Dionysius van der Sterre, who often had Erasmus as a guest between the latter's expeditions: *Zeer aanmerkelijke reysen gedaan door Jan Erasmus Reining, meest in de West-Indien en ook in veel andere deelen des werelds* (Amsterdam, 1691) [**123**].[14] This book makes clear that one of the salient features of life as a buccaneer was lack of food. Hunger was always just around the corner.

Curaçao's fast growth into one of the major entrepôts in the Western Hemisphere was due to the Dutch role in the international slave trade. Before the mid-seventeenth century, Dutch slave ships had mainly supplied New Holland in Brazil and some foreign islands in the Caribbean, but in the 1660s Spanish America was discovered as a market [**122**].[15]

The slaves were usually transported first to Curaçao and held there before embarking on the final leg of their odyssey from Africa. Only a few stayed behind on the island to work for the West India Company or, at a later stage, for private individuals. For decades, the Dutch had acted intermittently as sub-contractors of the *asiento*, the official Spanish government monopoly for supplying slaves to Spain's American colonies. When English and French slave traders assumed the lead in this ugly business, replacing the Dutch, Curaçao did not sink into oblivion. It had already become a prominent trading place in the Caribbean, essential especially to the economy of Venezuela. In an attempt to root out Dutch trade with this colony, Spanish authorities set up a rival commercial company, but it never managed to dislodge the Dutch completely [**138**].[16]

Smuggling and Prosperity

Dutch trade with the Spanish colonies could only take place secretly, since both states were officially committed to preventing commercial intercourse between their New World colonies. Violating the restrictions on a daily basis, Dutch merchants in America regularly sent large quantities of Spanish cocoa and tobacco to their mother country. Much about the organization of their illicit trade, which involved bribing guards and exchanging secret signs with Spanish merchants, can be learned from the log of the merchantmen *Arents Bergh*, covering the years 1714-15, which is kept in the John Carter Brown Library [**129**].

Housing construction in Willemstad, Curaçao's excellent port, was more or less adapted to com-

---

12 "Elaborate account of the French bragging at the Fort of Curaçao."

13 *De Americaensche zee-Roovers. Behelsende een pertinente en waerachtige beschrijving van alle de voornaemste Roveryen* ("The American pirates. Containing a pertinent and honest description of all main piracies"). Amsterdam, 1678.

14 "Very considerable voyages made by Jan Erasmus Reining, mostly in the West Indies and also in many other parts of the world."

15 *Pertinent en waarachtig verhaal van alle de handelingen en directie van Pedro van Belle, ontrent den slavenhandel* ("Pertinent and honest story about all acts and the directorship of Pedro van Belle relevant to the slave trade"). Rotterdam, 1689.

16 Real Compañía Guipuzcoana de Caracas, *Manifiesto, que con incontestables hechos prueba los grandes beneficios, que ha producido el establecimiento de la Real Compañia Guipuzcoana de Caracas* ("Manifesto, which proves with incontestable proof, the great benefits which the establishment of the Royal Guipuzcoan Company of Caracas has produced"). Madrid? 1749?

N

0   250 km

0   250 mi

Gulf
of
Mexico

FLORIDA

ATLANTIC

OCEAN

Bahamas

Matanzas

Cuba

Hispaniola

Jamaica

Puerto
Rico

St. Maarten

Saba
St. Eustatius

St. Christopher

Lesser Antilles

HONDURAS

Caribbean   Sea

Martinique

Barbados

Aruba   *Curaçao*
Bonaire

Punta de Araya

Tobago

PACIFIC
OCEAN

V E N E Z U E L A

Trinidad

Orinoco R.

GUIANAS

MAP VI   The Caribbean

merce. The houses, a Dutchman observed, "are mostly built of bricks, one or two stories high, according to the owner's means; downstairs are the warehouses or repositories, which are very convenient and comfortable; around the first floor there is a veranda, where in the heat of the day the occupants seat themselves for refreshment" [**148**].[17]

Curaçao's commercial character did not fail to leave its mark on the island's religious life. The practice of Roman Catholicism was probably allowed more leeway there than anywhere else in the Dutch colonial world. The Genoese "factors", or trading representatives, of the slave *asiento* already had a chapel of their own, and from an early date, under certain conditions, priests were allowed to hold Catholic services in the colony. The priests proved much more concerned about the spiritual welfare of African slaves than the Reformed ministers did. The attempts by the priests to convert blacks and mulattoes were so successful that it did not take long before Catholicism became the principal religion of Curaçao. The Reformed Church had only a small congregation of white men, who were not noted for leading pious lives.

The white elite also included a large group of Sephardic Jews, who had come from New Holland (Dutch Brazil) and Amsterdam to Curaçao in the middle of the seventeenth century. They settled as free planters on plots of land assigned to them by the director of the island. They could practice their religion unhindered and were protected in all possible ways by the West India Company. What is more, even unofficial antisemitism seems to have been a rare phenomenon in Curaçaoan society. Dominating certain professions, such as trade, insurance, and brokerage, the Jewish community was so successful that large sums of money could be raised to finance the construction of a new synagogue after the old one had become too small. The building, which was finished in 1732, is still the oldest functioning Jewish house of worship in the New World.

Few New World travellers visited Curaçao, but there were some exceptions. The account of a French traveller in the late eighteenth century is remarkable mainly for its questionable veracity. He claimed that there were no police on the island, and no system of justice, and that homicide and theft were rampant [**159**].[18] Curaçao may not have been a Garden of Eden, but these alleged characteristics fell wide of the mark. Still, peaceful in fact as the inhabitants may have been, Curaçao had its share of disagreements. West India Company officials and leading merchants were frequently at loggerheads with

each other, usually over the payment of taxes. In order to gain an insight into the problems, the Company sent two monitors to the island in 1789. They drew up a report on behalf of the stadholder, a manuscript copy of which is owned by the JCB [**161**].[19]

In the eighteenth century, Curaçao's position as the central entrepôt of the West Indies was gradually taken over by St. Eustatius. Its marketplace and the roads of Orange Bay were even more cosmopolitan than those of Willemstad in Curaçao. Lured by low customs duties, Englishmen, Frenchmen, North Americans, Spaniards, and Danes, as well as Dutchmen offered their merchandise for sale. The island's epithet "the Golden Rock" alludes to the lucrative trade in various products. Rum and molasses found a ready market, and by the 1770s St. Eustatius had become the main supplier of tea to the British continental colonies. With the coming of the War for Independence, it was not long before vessels loaded with arms followed the same route.

The trade in war supplies at St. Eustatius had already concerned the British government, but it was infuriated when news arrived about an incident that had occurred in November 1776. When a brigantine from the rebellious British colonies, the *Andrew Doria*, had appeared in Orange Bay flying the new Grand Union flag, it was saluted from the Dutch fort in the customary way offered to any sovereign nation. This seemingly inconsequential act was in fact tantamount to diplomatic recognition of the newly independent United States, making the United Provinces the first country to take this important step [**149**].[20] Four years went by before Britain took revenge. In February 1781, in the opening stages of the Fourth Anglo-Dutch War, an expedition

17 J.H. Hering, *Beschryving van het eiland Curaçao en de daar onder hoorende eilanden, Bon-Aire, Oroba en Klein Curaçao* ("Description of the island of Curaçao and the subordinate islands of Bonaire, Aruba and Little Curaçao"). Amsterdam, 1779.

18 Nicolas Louis Bourgeois, *Voyages intéressans dans différentes colonies françaises, espagnoles, anglaises* ("Interesting voyages in different French, Spanish, English colonies"). London and Paris, 1788.

19 *Raport aan Zijne Doorluchtigste Hoogheid den Heere Prince van Orange en Nassau &&& overgegeven van wegen Hoogst des Zelfs Commissarissen* ("Report to His Serene Highness, the Prince of Orange and Nassau &&& submitted by His Own Commissioners"). Ca. 1789.

20 *Missive van bewindhebberen der Westindische Compagnie, met een deductie door den commandeur van St. Eustatius* ("Missive of the directors of the West India Company, with a report by the commander of St. Eustatius"). 1779.

GEVECHT van 's LANDS SCHIP *MARS*, tegen de ENGELSCHE OORLOGSCHEPEN MONARCH, PANTHER en *SIJBILLE*.

FIG. 6.13 This Anglo-Dutch naval battle took place off St. Eustatius, just days before an English naval force in 1781 put an end to the island's prosperity. From Cornelius de Jong, *Reize naar de Caribische eilanden* (Haarlem, 1807).

led by Admiral Rodney rapidly forced the authorities on "Statia" to surrender, seized 150 vessels, and put the commerce of the island out of action for years to come. Dutch lieutenant Cornelius de Jong van Rodenburgh was held on the island as a prisoner of war and witnessed the destruction of the Golden Rock. He gave a full account in *Reize naar de Caribische eilanden, in de jaren 1780 en 1781* (Haarlem, 1807) [**169**].[21]

The Decline and Fall of the Company

From the moment it was founded, in 1674, the second West India Company was overshadowed by its older sister, the East India Company, or the VOC. Even the few monopolies that were left to it came under attack from a number of independent traders, mostly from Zeeland. The last monopoly was given up in the 1730s, when private traders were allowed to enter the slave trade. The main reason the Company yielded to their will was financial trouble, which went from bad to worse after the Dutch loss of the *asiento* sub-contracts. Stimulated by the uncurbed speculation of investors, new shares in the company had been issued in the wake of the War of the Spanish Succession (1701-1713), but this paper prosperity came to a quick and painful end, as it did in the rest of Europe.

Lacking the financial means to make the investments in commerce that were urgently needed, the Company found itself at a dead end. Company forts could no longer be maintained and ships were out of repair, which soon led to costly naval disasters. The crisis caused by the crash of the Surinamese plantation loans was harmful, too, since the Company was bound to keep the colony going, and with the need for continuing subsidies it soon reached the bottom of its treasury. The States General helped out once in a while, but eventually decided not to extend the patent when it expired in 1791. The colonies in Africa and the Americas, as well as the Company shares, now came under the administration of the States General, signaling the end of an era.

FIG. 6.14 Engraved title-page of Willem Bosman, *Nauwkeurige beschryving van de Guinese Goud-Tand en Slave-kust* (Utrecht, 1704): a view of a West African society. The slave trade from West Africa to the New World was a West India Company monopoly until the 1730s.

---

21 "Voyage to the Caribbean islands, in the years 1780 and 1781."

Epilogue

Dutch voyages to the Americas grew out of the protracted struggle between Spain and its rebellious provinces in the Netherlands. One of the motives underlying the first Dutch transatlantic expeditions was the wish to take bread out of the enemy's mouth by the bold design of seizing the silver mines of Mexico and Peru. This ambitious plan was never realized, but the Dutch did manage once, thanks to Piet Heyn's dashing exploit in 1628, to intercept the produce of the mines.

Another Dutch objective was colonization. Colonies were founded to provide an outlet for people willing to risk the hazards of travel and settlement in a New World, be it for economic reasons or to escape Old World constraints. Expectations were high, but the volume of migration even to Brazil or New Netherland, the largest colonies in the days of the first West India Company, was most disappointing.

Still, the Dutch left their mark on the Americas. The artistic representations of Brazil were unique, and scientific knowledge of the region of New Holland was not superseded before the nineteenth century. In the end, it was Dutch adaptability to the shifting trading configurations in the Atlantic that helped to make possible their substantial economic gains.

The Dutch in the Caribbean were content with their role of intermediaries. In the middle years of the seventeenth century, capital and technology from the Netherlands were instrumental in setting up the sugar industry of Barbados, Martinique, Guadeloupe, and St. Christopher. The English Navigation Acts and Colbert's mercantilist policies seemed to spell the end of the Dutch role as an intermediary, but the transit trade with foreign colonies helped them to survive. Through the islands of Curaçao and St. Eustatius, commercial relations were established with all parts of the Caribbean. This trade involved the exchange of European manufactures (imported from the Netherlands) for crops from non-Dutch colonies which were directed to the Dutch metropolis in large amounts.

Consequently, the commercial role of the Netherlands was more important than a look at a map of the Americas would suggest. After the Peace of Breda (1667), very little was left of the Dutch empire in the Americas. Brazil and New Netherland had both been abandoned and what remained was six small Caribbean islands and a string of colonies on the Wild Coast. The plantation colonies did not fare well, which was little wonder considering the odds they faced. While the East India Company was able to shift part of its overhead costs to consumers, the WIC's policy was not aimed at protecting crops imported from the Dutch colonies. At their home market, therefore, sugar and coffee from Suriname had to compete with tropical crops from other empires. It was precisely the Dutch "brokerage" in the Atlantic which underlay Company policy. As long as the Dutch had a large share in the carrying trade of foreign colonial crops, and as long as much Dutch capital was invested in foreign Caribbean plantation economies, protection for the products of Dutch colonies in particular was out of the question.

The English occupation of the early nineteenth century put an end to this mediating role. By the time the islands were returned to the Dutch, they had lost their function as regional markets, and their mercantile activities were limited to meeting the needs of their own populations. A resurgence of the transit trade never occurred.

The Dutch transit centers in the Caribbean, to some extent, were copies of the entrepôt of Amsterdam. In addition to this economic function, social institutions and traditions were transplanted from the United Provinces to the New World as well. The Dutch were to bequeath a tradition of tolerance to the Americas. The liberal traditions of the homeland turned Dutch colonies into oases in a desert of bigotry. In the mid-1640s, only twenty years after its foundation, New Amsterdam was home to eighteen different nationalities and a wide variety of religious groups. In Brazil, the reign of Johan Maurits underwrote tolerance of creeds other than Calvinism, thus providing a safe haven for Jews. Other Sephardim and Ashkenazim found refuge on the Caribbean islands and on the Wild Coast. Everywhere, however, Calvinism continued to be the official religion. In North America, the Dutch Reformed Church remained a pivotal social institution long after the English conquest. The role of the Church was much less pronounced in the Caribbean and circum-Caribbean colonies, which had been settled in the spirit of the buccaneer and never lost that birthmark.

One group of migrants to Dutch America was not looking for adventure, asylum, or opportunities for employment. Between 1600 and 1803, Dutch ships carried 543,000 African slaves across the Atlantic, half of whom ended up in the Dutch colonies, where slavery would not be abolished until 1863. The number may seem large, but it is estimated that 8 million Africans in total were brought to the Americas in the same time period. The major part of the present-day population of Suriname and the Dutch Antilles has African roots.

Slavery and the slave trade did not stigmatize Dutch exploits in the eyes of European Americans, since African bondage was almost universally accepted in the Atlantic world, indeed accepted globally. Most leaders of the independence movement in Spanish America, for instance, paid little more than lip service to abolitionism. And while they called for an end to Spanish "slavery," their actual aim was to finish off colonialism. In their struggle, some of the South American freedom fighters were inspired by the example of a brave people that shook off the Spanish yoke. They depicted the Netherlands as a paragon of heroism, of self-sacrificing indomitability. The political system that had come out of the war with the Habsburgs likewise served as a model, since it was one of the few republics history had produced, along with the city-states of antiquity and those of contemporary Italy. Dutch republican institutions were studied carefully, not only in nineteenth-century Spanish America but also in the Thirteen States. The *Plakkaat van Verlatinge*, the document that served as a proclamation of secession in the early stages of the Dutch war with Spain, inspired the authors of the Declaration of Independence. Throwing in their lot with the North Americans, the Dutch, for their part, expressed their sympathy in the salute at the Golden Rock, and the loans negotiated by John Adams laid the foundation of a continuous alliance of amity between both states.

Chronological List of Works in the Catalogue

COMPILED BY BURTON VAN NAME EDWARDS

[1] **Vespucci, Amerigo**, 1451-1512.

Van der nieuwer werelt oft landtscap nieuwelicx gheuo[n]de[n] va[n]de[n] doorluchtighe[n] con[inc]. van Portugael door de[n] alder beste[n] pyloet ofte zeekender d[er] werelt.

Gheprent Thantwerpen aen Dyseren waghe. Bi Ja[n] va[n] Doesborch. [1507?].

[2] **Ortelius, Abraham**, 1527-1598.

Theatrum orbis terrarum.

[Antwerp] Auctoris aere & cura impressum absolutumque apud Ægid. Coppenium Diesth, Antuerpiae, XX. Maii. M.D.LXX. [20 May 1570].

[3] **Casas, Bartolomé de las**, 1474-1566.

Seer cort verhael vande destructie van d'Indien vergadert deurden Bischop don fray Bartholome de las Casas, oft Casaus, van sinte Dominicus orden. In Brabantsche tale getrouwelick uyte Spaensche ouergeset.

[Antwerp?] 1578.

[4] **Casas, Bartolomé de las**, 1474-1566.

Spieghel der Spaenscher tyrannye in West Indien. Waer inne verhaelt wordt de moordadige, schandelijcke, ende grouwelijcke feyten, die de selve Spanjaerden gebruyckt hebben inde selve landen. ... In Spaenscher talen beschreuen, door den E. Bisschop don fray Bartholome de las Casas, van S. Dominicus oorden.

t'Amstelredam. By Nicolaes Biestkens de Jonge. Ende men vintse te coop by Cornelis Claesz. Opt water int schrijfboeck. 1596.

[5] **Linschoten, Jan Huygen van**, 1563-1611.

Itinerario, voyage ofte schipvaert, van Ian Huygen van Linschoten naer Oost ofte Portugaels Indien, inhoudende een corte beschryvinghe der selver landen ende zee-custen ... Alles beschreven ende by een vergadert, door den selfden ... voor alle curieuse ende liefhebbers van vreemdigheden.

t'Amstelredam. By Cornelis Claesz. op't vvater, in't schrijf-boeck, by de oude brugghe. Anno M.D.XCVI. [1596].

[6] **Acosta, José de**, 1540-1600.

Historie naturael ende morael van de Westersche Indien waer inne ghehandelt wordt van de merckelijckste dinghen des hemels, elementen, metalen, planten ende ghedierten van dien: als oock de manieren, ceremonien, wetten, regeeringen ende oorloghen der Indianen. Ghecomponeert door Iosephum de Acosta, der Jesuitscher oorden: ende nu eerstmael uyt den Spaenschen in onser Nederduytsche tale overgheset: door Ian Huyghen van Linschoten.

Tot Enchuysen, by Jacob Lenaertsz. Meyn, boeckvercooper, woonende op den hoeck van de kerck brugghe, int schrijfboeck. Anno 1598.

[7] **Veer, Gerrit de**.

Vraye description de trois voyages de mer tres admirables, faicts en trois ans, a chacun an un, par les navires d'Hollande et Zelande, au Nord par derriere Norvvege, Moscovie, et Tartarie, vers les royaumes de China & Catay: ensemble les decouvremens de VVaygat, Nova Sembla, & ... Groenlande ... par Girard Le Ver.

Imprimé a Amstelredam: par Cornille Nicolas, sur l'eaue, au livre a ecrire., Anno M.D.XCVIII. [1598].

[8] **Potgieter, Barent Jansz**, b. 1574.

VVijdtloopigh verhael van tgene de vijf schepen (die int jaer 1598. tot Rotterdam toegherust werden, om door de Straet Magellana haren handel te dryven) wedervaren is, tot den 7. september 1599. toe, op welcken dagh Capiteijn Sebald de Weert, met twee schepen, door onweder vande vlote versteken werdt. ... Meest beschreven door M. Barent Iansz, Cirurgijn.

t'Amsterdam, by Zacharias Heijns, inde Warmoestraet, inde hooft-dueghden. [1600].

[9] **Outghersz., Jan**, fl. 1600.

Nieuwe volmaeckte beschryvinghe der vervaerlijcker Straete Magellani ... beschreven worden, door Ian Outghersz. van Enchuysen, die de selve strate (stuerman zijnde op 'tschip 't Geloove genaemt) hen ende weder gezeylt, ende over de G. maenden daer in ghelegen heeft.

t'Amsterdam, by Zacharias Heyns, inde Warmoestraet inde hooft-dueghden. [1600].

[10] **Casas, Bartolomé de las**, 1474-1566.

Spieghel der Spaenscher tyrannye, in West-Indien. Waer inne verhaelt wordt de moordadighe, schandelijcke ende grouwelijcke feyten, die de selve Spaenjaerden ghebruyckt hebben inde selve landen. ... In Spaenscher talen beschreven, door den E. Bisschop Don Fray Bartholome de las Casas, van S. Dominicus oorden.

t'Amstelredam, by Cornelis Claesz. Boekvercooper woonende opt water, int schrijfboeck. Anno 1607.

[11] *Consideratien vande vrede in Nederlandt gheconcipieert, anno 1608.*

[Netherlands, 1608].

[12] *Dialogus oft tzamensprekinge, gemaect op den vrede-handel. Ghestelt by vraghe ende antwoorde. Overgheset wt de Fransche in onse Nederduytsche tale.*

[Netherlands] M.VI^c.VIII. [1608].

[13] *Discours by forme van remonstrantye: vervatende de noot-saeckelickheydt vande Oost-Indische navigatie, by middel vande vvelcke, de vrye Neder-landtsche provincien, apparent zijn te gheracken totte hoochste prosperiteyt ... Ende dit alles tot groote aensienlijcke heerschappie vande Hispaensche ende Portugesche natien, in deselve quartieren.*

[Netherlands] Ghedruckt anno 1608.

[14] **Usselincx, Willem**, 1567-1647?

Bedenckinghen over den staet van de vereenichde Nederlanden: nopende de zeevaert, coop-handel, ende de gemeyne neeringe inde selve. Ingevalle den peys met de aerts-hertogen inde aenstaende vrede-handlinge getroffen wert. Door een lief-hebber eenes oprechten ende bestandighen vredes voorghestelt.

[Netherlands] Gedruckt int jaer ons Heeren. 1608.

[15] **Usselincx, Willem**, 1567-1647?

Naerder bedenckingen, over de zee-vaerdt, coophandel ende neeringhe, als mede de versekeringhe vanden staet deser vereenichde landen, inde teghenwoordighe vrede-handelinghe met den coninck van Spangnien ende de aerts-hertoghen. Door een lies-hebber [sic] eenes oprechten, ende bestandighen vredes voorghestelt.

[Netherlands] Ghedruckt in het jaer ons Heeren 1608.

[16] **Usselincx, Willem**, 1567-1647?

Vertoogh, hoe nootwendich, nut ende profijtelick het sy voor de Vereenighde Nederlanden te behouden de vryheyt van te handelen op West-Indien, inden vrede metten Coninck van Spaignen.

[Netherlands, 1608].

[17] *Vanden spinnekop ende t'bieken ofte droom-ghedicht.*

[Netherlands, 1608].

[18] *Den Nederlandtschen bye-corf: waer ghy beschreven vint, al het gene dat nu uytgegaen is, op den stilstant ofte vrede ... beghinnende in mey 1607. ende noch en hebben wy het eynde niet. Ende is ghestelt op een t'samen-sprekinge, tusschen een Vlamyng ende Hollander. Noch is hier by ghevoecht, een ghedicht ter eeren des beghonnen peys, tusschen Phillippum den Derden van dien name coninck van Spaegnien, etc. ende de edele groot-moghende heeren Staten Generael vande Gheunieerde Provincien. Beschermt ons Heere. Int jaer sesthien hondert en acht, jeghelijck nae een goede vrede wacht.*

[Netherlands, 1608].

[19] **Veer, Gerrit de**.

The true and perfect description of three voyages, so strange and woonderfull, that the like hath neuer been heard of before ... by the ships of Holland and Zeland, on the North sides of Norway, Muscouia and Tartaria, towards the kingdomes of Cathaia & China; shewing the discouerie of the straights of Weigates, Noua Zembla, and ... Greenland ...

Imprinted at London: For T. Pauier. 1609

[20] **Langenes, Barent**.

Hand-boeck; of cort begrijp der caerten ende beschrijvinghen van alle landen des werelds. Van nieuvvs oversien ende vermeerdert.

't Amstelredam by Cornelis Claesz, op't water, in't schrijf-boeck. 1609.

[21] **Leubelfing, Johann von**.

Ein schön lustig Reissbuch, vor niemals in Truck kommen: darinnen begriffen, in was Gestalt, die Herren Staaden der Vnirten Niderländischen Provincien, ein Armada zugericht, vnd auff dem Meer die Jnsulen in Hispanien und West Jndien besuchen lassen. ... Gereist vnd fleissig beschriben, durch den gestrengen, edlen vnnd vesten Herrn, Johann von Leublfing ...

Getruckt zu Vlm, durch Johann Meder. M.DC.XII. [1612].

[22] **Spilbergen, Joris van**, 1568?-1620.

Copie van een brief van den heere Admirael Spil-berghen: inhoudende de voyage by hem gedaen door de Strate Magelanica, tot inde Zuydt-Zee, al waer hem bejeghent is de vlote van don Rodrigo de Mendosa daer hy mannelijcken tegen gevochten, ende de victorije behouden heeft. Ende voorts wat hem op die reyse wedervaren is tot inde Molucques toe.

Tot Def [sic], ghedruckt by In Andriessz. Boeck-vercooper aen't Marckt-velt in't Gulden A.B.C. 1617.

[23] **Ottsen, Hendrik**.

Iournael oft daghelijcx-register van de voyagie na Rio de Plata, ghedaen met het schip ghenoemt de Silveren Werelt, het welcke onder 't admiraelschap van Laurens Bicker, ende het bevel van Cornelis van Heems-kerck als commis die custen van Guinea versocht hebbende ... beschreven door den schipper daer op gheweest zijnde Hendrick Ottsen.

Tot Amsterdam by Michiel Colijn, boeck-vercooper op't vvater by de Oude-brugge int Huys-boeck. 1617.

[24] **Spilbergen, Joris van**, 1568?-1620.

t'Historiael journal, van tghene ghepasseert is van weghen drie schepen, ghenaemt den Ram, Schaep ende het Lam, ghevaren uyt Zeelandt vander stadt Camp-Vere naer d'Oost-Indien, onder t'beleyt van Ioris van Speilberghen, generael, anno 1601. Den 5. Mey, tot in t'eylant Celon, vervatende veel schoone gheschiedenissen, die by haer op dese reyse gheschiedt zijn, inden tijde van twee jaer, elff maenden, neghenthien daghen. Dese historie is verciert met seventhien vvelghesneden platen, daer in ghefigureert zijn eylanden, steden, kusten, havens, ghevechten op verscheyden plaetsen, met meer ander afbeeldinghen, als mede een heerlijcke beschryvinghe vanander landen, seer profijtelijck voor de Zeevarende man. Ghecorrigeert verbetert ende vermeerdert.

t'Amsterdam, by Michiel Colijn boeck-vercooper opt water, int Huysboeck aende Cooren-Marct. 1617.

[25] **Noort, Olivier van**, 1558 or 9-1627.

Beschrijvinge vande voyagie om den geheelen werelt-kloot, ghedaen door Olivier van Noordt van Vtrecht, generael over vier schepen ... te zeyl gegaen van Rotterdam den tweeden Julij 1598. Ende den generael met het schip Mauritius is alleen weder ghekeert in augusto, in't jaer onses Heeren 1601. ...

t'Amsterdam, by Michiel Colijn, boeckverkooper op't vvater, aen de Koorn-Marct, in t' Huys-Boeck. Ao 1618.

[26] **Schouten, Willem Corneliszoon**, d. 1625.

Iournal ofte beschryvinghe van de wonderlicke reyse, ghedaen door Willem Cornelisz Schouten van Hoorn, inde jaren 1615. 1616. en 1617. Hoe hy bezuyden de Strate van Magellanes een nieuwe passagie tot inde groote Zuydzee ontdeckt, en voort den gheheelen aerdkloot omgheseylt, heeft. Wat Eylanden, vreemde volcken en wonderlicke avontueren hem ontmoet zijn.

t'Amsterdam, by Willem Jansz, op't water inde Sonnewyser, 1618.

[27] **Schouten, Willem Corneliszoon**, d. 1625.

Diarium vel descriptio laboriosissimi, & molestissimi itineris, facti à Guilielmo Cornelii Schoutenio Hornano. Annis 1615. 1616. & 1617. Cum à parte australi freti Magellanici, novum ductum, aut fretum, in Magnum Mare Australe detexit, totumq[ue] orbem terrarum circumnavigavit. Quas insulas, & regiones, & populos viderit, & quae pericula subierit.

Amsterdami, apud Petrum Kaerium. Ao. 1619.

[28] **Spilbergen, Joris van**, 1568?-1620.

Oost ende West-Indische spiegel der nieuvve navigatien, daer in vertoont vverdt de leste reysen ghedaen door Ioris van Speilbergen, admirael van dese vloote; in vvhat manieren hy de VVereldt rontsom gheseylt heeft.

Tot Leyden, by Nicolaes van Geelkercken, Anno 1619.

[29] **Avontroot, Johannes**, ca. 1563-1632.

Den grouwel der verwoestinghe, oft grondich bericht ende ontdeckinghe, van de gronden der Spaensche Inquisitie. Tot waerschouwinghe van alle goede ende oprechte Nederlanders ende evangelische gheloofsghenoten. Wtgheghven door een vriendts ende liefhebber der selver. Hier is oock noch by ghevoecht de Spaensche Inquisitie, beschreven door Reginaldum Gonsalvium Montanum, comt ick sal u toonen uwen vyandt.

In s'Graven-Haghe. By Aert Meuris, boeckvercooper inde Papestraet in den Bybel, Anno 1621.

[30] **United Provinces of the Netherlands. Staten Generaal.**

Octroy, by de hooghe mogende heeren Staten Generael, verleent aende West-Indische Compagnie, in date den derden Junii 1621.

In s'Graven-Haghe, by Hillebrant Iacobssz, ordinaris ende ghesworen drucker vande ed: mo: heeren Staten van Hollandt en[de] VVest-Vrieslandt. Anno 1621.

[31] *More excellent observations of the estate and affaires of Holland. In a discourse, shewing how necessarie and conuenient it is for their neighbouring countries, as well as the Netherland Prouinces, to trade into the West Indies. And by most vrgent and good reasons, prouing that by the West Jndian trade now erected in Holland, the said company shall receiue great benefit, the Hollanders greater seruice, and the Spaniard more hurt, and greater disaduantage then [sic] euer be receiued before. As also the great profit and commodity the said Netherlands haue reaped and receiued, during the time of 24. yeares that the said Company hath traded into the East Indies. Faithfully translated out of the Dutch copie.*
Printed at London, by E.A. for Nicholas Bourne and Thomas Archer, and are to be sold at their shops at the exchange, and the Popes-head Pallace. 1622.

[32] **Usselincx, Willem**, 1567-ca. 1647.

Korte onderrichtinghe ende vermaeninge aen alle liefhebbers des vaderlandts, om liberaljcken te teeckenen inde West-Indische Compagnie: in de vvelcke kortelijck wort aenghewesen, de nootsaeckelijckheyt, doenljckheyt ende nuttcheyt van de selve. Door een liefhebber des vaderlandts inghestelt, ende tot ghemeyne onderrichtinghe in druck vervoordert.

Tot Leyden: inde druckerye van Isaack Elzevier, boeck-drucker vande Universiteyt, Anno 1622.

[33] *Reys-boeck van het rijcke Brasilien, Rio de la Plata ende Magallanes, daer in te sien is, de gheleghentheyt van hare landen ende steden, haren handel ende wandel, met de vruchten ende vruchbaerheyt der selver: alles met copere platen uytghebeelt. Als oock de leste reyse van den Heer van Dort, met het veroveren vande Baeye de Todos los Santos, tsamen ghestelt door N.G.*

[Dordrecht?] Ghedruckt int jaer onses heeren, anno 1624. By Ian Canin.

[34] *Steyger-praetjen, tusschen Ian Batavier en Maetroos, over het apprehenderen van den Gouverneur ende Provinciael van gantsch Brasilien, met haer geselschap.*

'Amstelredam, by Claes Jansz Visscher. Anno 1624.

[35] **Corrêa, João de Medeiros**, d. 1671.

Relaçam verdadeira de tudo o succedido na restauração da Bahia de Todos os Sanctos desde o dia, em que partirão as armadas de Sua Magestade, té o em que em a dita cidade foraõ aruorados seus estandartes com grande gloria de Deos, exaltaçaõ do rey, & reyno, nome de seus vassallos, que nesta empresa se acharaõ, anihilaçaõ, & perda dos rebeldes Olandezes ali domados. ...

Em Lisboa. Por Pedro Craesbeeck impressor del rey, anno 1625. Vendese na rua noua na tenda de Paulos Crasbeeck. [1625].

[36] **Guerreiro, Bartolomeu**, 1564-1642.

Iornada dos vassalos da coroa de Portugal, pera se recuperar a cidade do Saluador, na Bahya de Todos os Santos, tomada pollos olandezes, a oito de mayo de 1624. & recuperada ao primeiro de mayo de 1625. Feita pollo padre Bertolameu Guerreiro da Companhia de Iesu.

Em Lisboa. Por Mattheus Pinheiro. Anno de 1625. Impressa à custa de Francisco Aluarez liureiro. Vendese em sua casa, defronte da Misericordia. [1625].

[37] **Laet, Joannes de**, 1593-1649.

Nieuvve wereldt ofte beschrijvinghe van West-Indien, wt veelderhande schriften ende aen-teeckeninghen van verscheyden natien by een versamelt door Ioannes de Laet, ende met noodighe kaerten ende tafels voorsien.

Tot Leyden, in de druckerye van Isaack Elzevier. Anno 1625.

[38] **United Provinces of the Netherlands. Staten Generaal.**

Placcaet ende ordonnantie vande Hoge ende Mog: heeren Staten Generael der Vereenichde Nederlanden, tegens Wechloopers die hun indienst vande West-Indische Compaignie begeven hebbende, verloopen, ofte ooc in tijt van noot haer schepe[n] verlaten.

In s'Graven-Haghe, by de weduwe, ende erfghenamen van wijlen Hillebrant Iacobssz van Wouw, ordinaris druckers vande Ho: Mo: heeren Staten Generael, Anno 1625.

[39] *Iournael vande Nassausche vloot, ofte beschryvingh vande voyagie om den gantschen aerdt-kloot, ghedaen met elf schepen: onder't beleyd vanden Admirael Iaques L'Heremite, ende Vice-Admirael Geen Huygen Schapenham, inde jaeren 1623, 1624, 1625, en 1626. ...*

t'Amsterdam, by Hessel Gerritsz ende Iacob Pietersz Wachter. 't Iaer 1626.

[40] **Willemssz, Salomon**.

Rapport gedaen aen Hare Ho, Mo. ende Sijn Excell. van den Capiteyn Salomon Willemssz, over 't ver-overen vande Silver-Vlote, komende van Nova Hispania, door 't beleyt van den Heer General Pieter Pieterssz Heyn.

In 's Graven-Haghe, by de VVeduwe, ende erfghen-amen van wijlen Hillebrant Iacobssz van VVouw, ordinaris druckers vande Ho. Mo. Heeren Staten Generael. Anno 1628.

[41] **Eibergen, Rutgerus**, fl. 1629.

Svvymel-klacht des Spaenschen conincks Phillipi Quarti, over het eerste verlies van sijn silver-vlote: waer mede dese landen, door Gods hulpe, verrijckt heeft den moedighen en manhaften zee-ridder, en generael Pieter Pietersen Heyn ...

t'Amstelredam, voor Willem Iansz Stam, boeckver-cooper inde Warmoesstraet, inde Hoochduytsche Bybel, M.DC.XXIX. [1629].

[42] *Eroberung der reiche silber-vloot inde bay oder haven Matancae. An 1628. den 8. Sept.*

[Amsterdam? ca. 1629].

[43] *Practiicke van den Spaenschen aes-sack: aen-gevvesen op de veroveringe, en victorie van den loffelijcken, voorsienighen, manlijck-hertighen Heer Generael Pieter Pietersz. Heyn. Met by-voeginghe van noodighe poëtische 't samen-spraecke; ende aerdi-ge rijm-vyeren, en vvellekomsten. Mitsgaders eenighe treur-versen op het droevich ongheluck des Coninckl: M: van Bohemen.*

In 's Gravenhage, gedruckt in't jaer ons heeren, 1629.

[44] *Rym-vieren op de ieghen-woordige victorie, bekomen door den manhaften Generael Pieter Pietersz. Heyn, van Delffs-Haven, in de veroveringe van de Spaensche silvere-vlote, onder 't Eylandt Cubæ, anno 1628. Daer-by-gevvought, eenige treur-versen, over het drouvigh ongheluck, voor vveynigh dagen, sijne Co: Mat: van Bohemen over-ghekomen.*

[The Hague: Anthonis Iansz. Tongerloo, 1626].

[45] **Spranckhuysen, Dionysius**, d. 1650.

Triumphe van vveghen de gheluckighe ende over-rijcke victorie vvelcke de Heere Onse God op den 8. en septembris des jaers 1628. verleent heeft aen de vlote vande VVest-Indische Compagnie, onder het beleydt vanden Heer Generael Pieter Pietersz. Heyn, teghen de silver-vlote onser vyanden, komende van Nova Hispania, in en omtrent de haven van Matançe. Beschreven door Dionysium Spranckhuysen.

Tot Delf, ghedruckt by Jan Andriesz. Kloeting, boeck-ver-cooper aen 't Marckt-veldt in't Gulden A,B,C., Anno 1629.

[46] **Baardt, Pieter**.

Petri Baardt Friesche Triton. Over t'geluckich veroveren van de Stercke Stadt Olinda, met alle de forten in Fernambucq. Gegeven ten tryumph-dage aende E. Hoog-Mog. Heren Staten Generael, den doorluchtigen Prince van Orangien, ende de bewint-hebberen van de West-Indische Compagnie in de Ver-eenigde Nederlanden.

Ghedruckt tot Leeuwarden, by Claude Fonteyne, boeck-drucker ordinaris der Heren Staten van Frieslandt. Anno M.DC.XXX. [1630].

[47] **Baers, Johannes**, d. 1653.

Olinda, ghelegen int landt van Brasil, inde capitania van Phernambuco, met mannelijcke dapperheyt ende groote cour017e inghenomen, ende geluckelijck verovert op den 16. Februarij Ao. 1630. Onder het beleydt vanden seer manhaften ende cloeckmoedigen zee-helt, den Heere Henrick Lonck, gene-rael weghen de geoctroyeerde West-Indische Compagnie, over een machtige vloote schepen, door den VVel-Edelen, seer gestren-gen ende grootmoedige[n] Heere Diederich van Weerdenburg, Heere van Lent, Velt-Overste ende Colonel over dry Regimenten Infanterie. Cort ende claer beschreven, door Joannem Baers, dienaer des Godlijcken VVoorts inde heerlijckheyt van Vreeswijck, gheseyt de vaert, als een sichtbaer ghetuyge, int vijftichste jaer syns ouderdoms.

Ghedruckt tot Amsterdam, Voor Hendrick Laurentsz. boeck-vercooper op 't water. int schrijf-boeck, Anno 1630.

[48] *Die Stat Olinda de Phernambuco welche durch die Hollander im Februari 1630 erobert worden ...*

[Amsterdam, 1630].

[49] *Redenen, waeromme dat de Vereenighde Nederlanden, geensints eenighe vrede met den koningh van Spaignien konnen, mogen, noch behooren te maecken. Zijnde het tweede deel van 't Tractaet tegens pays, treves, en onderhandelinge met den koningh van Spaignien.*

In 's Graven-Hage, by Aert Meuris, boeckverkooper in de Papestraet in den Bybel, Anno 1630.

[50] **West Indische Compagnie (Netherlands)**

Articulen, met approbatie vande Ho: Mog: Heeren Staten Generael der Vereenichde Nederlanden, provisioneelijc beraemt by bewinthebberen van de generale geoctroyeerde West-Indische Compagnie, ter vergaderinge vande negenthiene, over het open ende vry stellen vanden handel ende negotie op de stadt Olinda de Parnambuco, ende custen van Brazil. Hier zijn achter by ghedruckt de Vryheden van Nieu-Nederlant.

t'Amstelredam, gedruckt voor Marten Iansz. Brant, boeck-verkooper by de Nieuwe Kerck, inde gerefor-meerde Catechismus, Anno 1631.

[51] **Blaeu, Willem Janszoon**, 1571-1638.

Tweede deel van 't Tooneel des aerdriicx, ofte Nieuwe atlas, uytgegeven door Wilhelm: en Iohannem Blaeu.

Amstelodami, apud Guiljelmum et Iohannem Blaeu. Anno MDCXXXV. [1635].

[52] *Vertoogh by een lief-hebber des vaderlants vertoont. Teghen het ongefondeerde ende schadelijck sluyten der vryen handel in Brazil.*

[The Hague?] In't jaer ons Heeren, M.DC.XXXVII. [1637].

[53] **Casas, Bartolomé de las**, 1474-1566.

Den spieghel der Spaense tyrannye, geschiet in West-Indien. Waer in te sien is de onmen[sc]helicke wreede feyten der Spangi[a]erden ... In't Spaens beschreven, door den E. Bisschop Don Fraes [sic] Bartholome de las Casas van S. Dominicus oorden. ...

Anno 1638. t'Amsterdam: gedrukt bij Evert Kloppenburg, op 't water tegen over de Koren Beurs inde Vergulden Bijbel.

[54] *Bril-gesicht voor de verblinde eyghen baetsuchtige handelaers op Brasil. By forme van advijs door een lief-hebber van 't vader-landt geschreven aen synen vriendt.*

[Amsterdam?] Gedruckt na de geboorte ons Heeren en Salighmakers Jesu Christi, op het jaer 1638.

[55] *Het spel van Brasilien, vergheleken by een goedt verkeer-spel.* [Amsterdam?], Ghedruckt in't iaer ons Heeren 1638.

[56] **Mercator, Gerhard**, 1512-1594.

Gerardi Mercatoris et I. Hondii. Atlas novus, sive descriptio geographica totius orbis terrarum, tabulis aeneis luculentis-simis & accuratissimis exornata, tribus tomis distinctus.

Amstelodami apud Ioannem Ianssonium & Henricum Hondium. 1638.

[57] **West Indische Compagnie (Netherlands)**

Reglement byde VVest-Indische Compagnie, ter vergaderinge vande negentiene, met approbatie vande Ho: Mo: Heeren Staten Generael, over het openstellen vanden handel op Brasil provisioneel ghearresteert. West-Indische Compagnie.

In 's Graven-haghe, byde weduwe, ende erfghenamen van wijlen Hillebrandt Iacobssz van Wouw, ordinaris druckers vande Ho: Mo: Heeren Staten Generale., Anno 1638.

[58] *Translaet uyt den Spaenschen, weghens 't gevecht tusschen des conincx silver vloot, en den Admirael Houte-been in West-Indien op den 31 Augustus 1638. 12 mylen van de Havana. Midtsgaders. De lyste van de dooden ende ghequeste die op des conincx Armade geweest zijn.*

[Amsterdam]: Eerst gedruckt in Spaensch tot Calis door Fernando Rey. Anno 1639. Ende nu t'Amstelredam gedruckt voor Francooys Lieshout, boeck-verkooper op den Dam, in't Groot-Boeck, Anno. 1639.

[59] **Moris, Gedeon.**

Copye. Van 't journael gehouden by Gedeon Moris, koopman op het schip vande West-Indische Compagnie, genaemt de Princesse, uytgevaren naer Bresilien van Zeelandt den 27 Februarij 1640. daer capiteyn op is Pieter Constant van Middelburg. Gesonden uyt Poortlant in Engelant aende kamer van Zeelandt per missive in dato 2 Martij 1640.…

t'Amsterdam, voor Francois Lieshout, boeckverkooper op den Dam in 't Groot-Boeck, anno 1640.

[60] **Guelen, Auguste de.**

Kort verhael vanden staet van Fernanbuc … Door Augustus van Quelen. Wt het Francois int Nederduytsch vertaelt.

t'Amsterdam, ghedruckt in't jaer ons Heeren, 1640.

[61] **Udemans, Godefridus**, ca. 1580-1649.

't Geestelyck roer van't coopmans schip, dat is: trouwbericht, hoe dat een coopman, en coopvaerder, hem selven dragen moet in syne handelinge, in pays, ende in oorloge, voor God, ende de menschen, te water ende te lande, insonderheydt onder de heydenen in Oost ende West-Indien: ter eeren Gods, stichtinge syner gemeynten, ende saligheyt syner zielen: mitsgaders tot het tijtlick welvaren van het vaderlandt, ende syne familie, door Godefridum Vdemans, bedienaer des H. Evangelii tot Ziericzee. Den tweeden druck, verbetert ende vermeerdert by den autheur. Met twee gherieffelijcke registers.

Tot Dordrecht, voor Françoys Boels, boeck-verkooper, wonende in de witte gekroonde Duyff, by't Stadthuys. Anno 1640 [i.e. 1641].

[62] **Grotius, Hugo**, 1583-1645.

Hugonis Grotii De origine gentium Americanarum dissertatio altera, adversus obtrectatorem …

Parisiis, apud Sebastianum Cramoisy, architypographum regium, viâ Iacobæâ, sub ciconiis. MDCXLIII. [1643].

[63] **Laet, Joannes de**, 1593-1649.

Ioannis de Laet Antwerpiani Notæ ad dissertationem Hugonis Grotii De origine gentium Americanarum et obser-vationes aliquot ad meliorem indaginem difficillimæ illius quæstionis.

Amstelodami, apud Ludovicum Elzivirium. MDCXLIII. [1643].

[64] *Aenwysinge: datmen vande Oost en West-Indische Compagnien, een compangie [sic] dient te maken. Mitsgaders twintich consideratien op de trafyque, zeevaert en commertie deser landen …*

In's Graven-Haghe, gedruckt by Ian Veeli, boeck-verkooper in de Gortstraet, 1644.

[65] **Augspurger, Johann Paul.**

Johann Paul Augspurgers kurtze und warhaffte Beschreibung der See-Reisen von Amsterdam in Holland nacher Brasilien in America, und Angola in Africa. Vom 4. Novembris 1640. biss 10. Julii 1642.…

Schleusingen, gedruckt bey Joh. Michael Schalln. Im Jahr 1644.

[66] **Laet, Joannes de, 1593-1649.**

Historie ofte Iaerlijck verhael van de verrichtinghen der Geoctroyeerde West-Indische Compagnie, zedert haer begin, tot het eynde van 't jaer sesthien-hondert ses-en-dertich; begrepen in derthien boecken, ende met verscheyden koperen platen verciert: beschreven door Ioannes de Laet …

Tot Leyden, by Bonaventuer ende Abraham Elsevier, Anno 1644.

[67] *Discours op verscheyde voorslaghen rakende d'Oost en UUest-Indische trafyken. Het eerste deel. Waerinne ghehandelt wert van't prolongeren of vernieuwen van't Oost-Indische octroy.*

[The Hague?] Gedruckt int Iaer ons Heeren 1645.

[68] *Iournael ofte kort discours, nopende de rebellye ende verra-delijcke desseynen der Portugesen, alhier in Brasil voorgenomen, 't welck in Junio 1645. is ondeckt. Ende wat vorder daer nae ghepasseert is, tot den 28. April 1647. Beschreven door een lief-hebber, dieselfs int begin der rebellye daer te lande is gheweest, ende aldaer noch is residerende.*

Tot Arnhem, ghedruckt by Jan Jacobsz. boeck-verkooper woonende in de Backer-straet, in de vergulde Persse, anno 1647.

[69] **Brouwer, Hendrick**, 1581 or 2-1643.

Journael ende historis verhael van de reyse gedaen by oosten de straet le Maire, naer de custen van Chili, onder het beleyt van den Heer Generael Hendrick Brouwer, inden jare 1643 voor gevallen, vervatende der Chilesen manieren, handel ende ghewoonten. Als mede Een beschryvinghe van het eylandt Eso, ghelegen ontrent dertigh mylen van het machtigh rijcke van Japan, op de hooghte van 39 graden, 49 minuten, noorder breete; soo alst eerst in 't selvige jaer door het schip Castricom bezeylt is. Alles door een liefhebber uyt verscheyden journalen ende schriften te samen gestelt.…

Tot Amsterdam, gedruckt by Broer Jansz, woonende op de Nieu-zijds Achter-burghwal, inde Silvere kan. Anno 1646.

[70] *Manifest door d'inwoonders van Parnambuco uytghegeven tot hun verantwoordinghe op 't aennemen der wapenen teghens de West-Indische Compagnie; ghedirigeert aen alle Christene Princen, ende besonderlijck aen de Hoogh-Mo. HH. Staten Generael van de vereenighde Nederlanden. Ghedruckt ende uyt het Portughies overgheset in onse Nederduytsche tale.*

[Netherlands] Anno 1646.

[71] **Baerle, Caspar van**, 1584-1648.

Casparis Barlæi, rerum per octennium in Brasilia et alibi nuper gestarum, sub præfectura illustrissimi Comitis I. Mauritii, Nassoviæ, &c. comitis, nunc Vesaliæ gubernatoris & equitatus foederatorum Belgii ordd. sub Auriaco ductoris, historia.

Amstelodami, ex typographeio Ioannis Blaeu, MDCXLVII. [1647].

[72] *De Brasilsche breede-byl; ofte t'samen-spraek, tusschen Kees Jansz. Schott, komende uyt Brasil, en Jan Maet, koopmans-knecht, hebbende voor desen ook in Brasil geweest, over den verloop in Brasil.*

[Amsterdam?] In't jaer onses heeren, 1647.

[73] *Brasilsche gelt-sack. Waer in dat claerlijck vertoont wordt, waer dat de participanten van de West-Indische Comp. haer gelt ghebleven is.*

Gedruct in Brasilien op't Reciff in de Bree-Bijl. [i.e. Amsterdam?] Anno 1647.

[74] **Lief-hebber**.

Claar vertooch van de verradersche en vyantlijcke acten en proceduren van Poortugaal, in't verwecken ende stijven van de rebellie ende oorloghe in Brasil. Beweesen uyt de brieven en geschriften van het selve Rijck ende hare ministers, door een lief-hebber by een versamelt, tot wederlegginge van de frivole excusen tot der Portugijsen onschult voort gebracht.

t' Amsterdam, gedruckt by de weduwe van Ioost Broersz. woonende in de Pijl-steegh, in de boeck-druck-erye, 1647.

[75] **Plante, Franciscus**.

Francisci Plante Brugensis Mauritiados libri xii. Hoc est: rerum ab illustrissimo heroe Ioanne Mauritio, comite Nassauiae &c. in Occidentali Indiâ gestarum descriptio poetica.

Lugduni Batavorum, Ex officina Ioannis Maire., Anno MDCXLVII. Vaeneunt Amsterodami apud Ioannem Blavium. [1647].

[76] *Brandt in Brasilien.*

[Netherlands?] Gedruct in't jaer ons Heeren, 1648.

[77] **Calado, Manuel**, 1584-1654.

O valeroso Lucideno. E triumpho da liberdade. Primeira parte. Composta por o p. mestre frei Manoel Calado …

Em Lisboa. Por Paulo Craesbeeck, impressor, & liureiro das Orde[n]s Militares. Anno do Senhor de 1648.

[78] *Eenige advijsen ende verklaringhen uyt Brasilien. In dato den 19. Mey 1648. Van't gepasseerde.*

Tot Amsterdam [i.e. The Hague], by Philips van Macedonien, drucker inde druckerije van Ian Roonpoorts Toorn. [i.e. L. Breeckevelt], Anno 1648.

[79] **Piso, Willem**, 1611-1678.

Historia naturalis Brasiliae, auspicio et beneficio illustriss. I. Mauritii Com. Nassau … adornata in qua non tantum plantæ et animalia, sed et indigenarum morbi, ingenia et mores descri-buntur et iconibus supra quingentas illustrantur.

Lugdun. Batavorum, apud Franciscum Hackium, et Amstelodami, apud Lud. Elzevirium. 1648.

[80] **Onpartydich toe-hoorder**.

Brasyls schuyt-praetjen, ghehouden tusschen een officier, een domine, en een coopman, noopende den staet van Brasyl: mede hoe de officieren en soldaten tegenwoordich aldaer ghetracteert werden, en hoe men placht te leven ten tyde doen de Portogysen noch onder het onverdraeghlijck iock der Hollanderen saten. Dit door een onpartydich toe-hoorder gheannoteert.

Ghedruckt inde West-Indische Kamer [i.e. The Hague?] by Maerten [i.e. F. Breeckevelt?], daer het gelt soo lustich klinckt alsser zijn aep-staerten. Anno 1649.

[81] **Schouten, Willem Corneliszoon**, d. 1625.

Iournael ofte beschryving vande wonderlijcke voyagie, ghedaen door VVillem Cornelisz Schouten, van Hoorn, in den Iaere 1615, 1616, ende 1617. Hoe hy bezuyden de Straete van Magellanes, een nieuwe passagie ontdeckt, en de geheele aerd-cloot om-gezeylt heeft.

Tot Dockum. Gedruckt by Louis Vlas-bloem, boeckdruck-er wonende inde Kerc Straet int Schrijf-boeck, 1649.

[82] *Amsterdamsche veerman op Middelburgh.*

Tot Vlissingen, Gedruckt by my Jacob Jansz Pieck, in't jaer ons Heeren. 1650.

[83] *'t Hollandts rommelzootje, vertoonende de gantsche gele-gentheyd van het benaaudt, ontzet, en gewapent Amsterdam.*

[Amsterdam?] Gedruckt op de pars, In 't jaar der Snaphaanen. [1650].

[84] **Broeck, Matheus van den**.

Journael, ofte historiaelse beschrijvinge van Matheus vanden Broeck. Van 't geen hy selfs ghesien ende waerachtigh gebeurt is, wegen 't begin ende revolte van de Portugese in Brasiel, als mede de conditie en het overgaen van de forten aldaer.

't Amstelredam, Voor Gerrit van Goedesbergen, boeck-verkooper op het water, by de nieuwe-brugh, inde Delfte Bybel. Anno 1651.

[85] *Beschrijvinghe van Virginia, Nieuw Nederlandt, Nieuw Engelandt, en d'Eylanden Bermudes, Berbados, en S. Christoffel. Dienstelijck voor elck een derwaerts handelende, en alle voort-planters van nieuw colonien. Met kopere figuren verciert.*

t'Amsterdam, By Joost Hartgers, boeck-verkooper op den Dam, bezyden't Stadt-huys, op de hoeck vande Kalver-straet, inde Boeck-winckel, Anno 1651.

[86] *Vertoogh, over den toestant der West-Indische Compagnie, in haer begin, midden, ende eyende, met een remedie tot redres van deselve. Eerste deel.*

Gedruct tot Rotterdam, by Iohannes van Roon, bouck-verkooper op de Leuve-have, in't Musijck-boeck. 1651.

[87] **Visscher, Nicolaes**, 1618-1679.

Novi Belgii Novaeque Angliae nec non partis Virginiae tabula multis in locis emendata a Nicolao Joannis Visschero.

[Amsterdam, ca. 1651].

[88] **Schoppe, Sigismund van**.

Copie, van den brief geschreven by Sigismund van Shoppe …

aen Hare Hog. Mog. de Heeren Staten Generael der Vereenigde Nederlanden; al waer hy, Schoppe, in vertoont, den miserabilen staet van de voornoemde Brasilien als mede, Klagende over de slechte assistentie, tot onderhoud van de militie; ende de onwilligheyd der oude soldaten.

Tot Middelburg, by Simon de Klager, woonende op de Haven, in de Hoop vol Patientie, anno 1654.

[89] **Portugal. Treaties**, etc. United Provinces of the Netherlands 1654 Jan. 26.

Accoord van Brasilien, mede van 't Recif, Maurits-Stadt, ende de omleggende forten van Brasil.

t'Amsterdam, By Claes Lambrechtsz. van der Wolf, 1654.

[90] *Cort, bondigh ende waerachtigh verhael van 't schandelijck overgeven ende verlaten vande voorname conquesten van Brasil, onder de regeeringe vande Heeren Wouter van Schonenburgh, president, Hendrick Haecx, hoogen raet, ende Sigismondus van Schoppe, luytenant Generael over de militie, 1654.*

Tot Middelburgh, gedruckt by Thomas Dircksz van Brouwers-haven, Anno 1655.

[91] ***Donck, Adriaen van der**, 1620-1655.*

Beschryvinge van Nieuvv-Nederlant, (ghelijck het tegenwoordigh in staet is) begrijpende de nature, aert, gelegentheyt en vrucht-baerheyt van het selve lant; mitsgaders de proffijtelijcke ende gewenste toevallen, die aldaer tot onderhout der menschen, (soo uyt haer selven als van buyten ingebracht) gevonden worden. Als mede de maniere en onghemeyne eygenschappen vande wilden ofte naturellen vanden lande. Ende een bysonder verhael vanden wonderlijcken aert ende het weesen der bevers, daer noch by gevoeght is een discours over de gelegentheyt van Nieuw Nederlandt, tusschen een Nederlandts patriot, ende een Nieuw Nederlander. Beschreven door Adriaen vander Donck, beyder rechten doctoor, die teghenwoordigh noch in Nieuw Nederlant is.

t'Aemsteldam, by Evert Nieuwenhof, boeck-verkooper, woonende op't Ruslandt in 't Schrijf-boeck, Anno 1655.

[92] **Vries, David Pietersz. de**, fl. 1593-1655.

Korte historiael, ende journaels aenteyckeninge, van verscheyden voyagiens in de vier deelen des wereldts-ronde, als Europa, Africa, Asia, ende Amerika gedaen, door D. David Pietersz. de Vries, artillerij-meester vande Ed: M: Heeren gecommitteerde raden van Staten van West-Vrieslandt ende 't Noorder-quartier. Waer in verhaelt werd wat batailjes hy te water gedaen heeft: yder landtschap zijn gedierte, gevogelt, wat soorte van vissen, ende wat wilde menschen naer 't leven geconterfaeyt, ende van de bosschen ende ravieren met haer vruchten.

t'Hoorn, voor David Pietersz. de Vries, artillerij-meester van't Noorder-quartier. Tot Alckmaer, by Symon Cornelisz. Brekegeest, Anno 1655.

[93] **Paräupába, Antonio.**

Twee verscheyden remonstrantien ofte vertogen, overgegeven aen Hare Ho: Mo: de Heeren Staten Generael der Vereenighe Nederlanden. Door Anthonio Paräupába ... Ende met het laetste ongeluckigh verlies vau [sic] Brazyl, vande gantsche Braziliaensche natie afgesonden; aen Hare Ho: Mo: om derselver natie erbermelijcken eñ jammerlijcken toestaut [sic] te vertonen, ende met eenen hulpe ende bystant te versoecken.

In's Graven-hage, gedruckt by Henricus Hondius, woonende inde Hofstraet, inde nieuwe konst-en-boeck-druckery. 1657.

[94] **O.K. (Otto Keye).**

Het waere onderscheyt tusschen koude en warme landen ... Voor-gestelt en vergeleken met Nieu-Nederlant, als sijnde een koudt landt en Guajana sijnde een warm landt, en beyde gelegen in America, doch onder een besonder climaet, en dat by gelegentheyt van de bevolckinge dewelcke tegenwoordig in beyde die gewesten wort gedaen. ... Door O.K.

In's Graven-Hage, gedruct voorden autheur, by Henricus Hondius, in de nieuwe konst-en-boeck-druckery, in de Hof-Straet. [1659].

[95] **Steendam, Jacob**, 1616-1672 or 3.

Klacht van Nieuw-Amsterdam, in Nieuw-Nederlandt, tot haar moeder: van haar begin, wasdom en tegenwoordigen stand.

t'Amsterdam, by Pieter Dircksz. Boeteman, boeck-drucker, op de Egelantiers-gracht. 1659.

[96] **Baerle, Caspar van**, 1584-1648.

Casparis Barlæi rerum per octennium in Brasilia et alibi gestarum, sub præfectura illustrissimi Comitis I. Mauritii Nassaviæ &c. comitis, historia. ... Editio secunda.

Clivis, ex officinâ Tobiæ Silberling, M.DC.LX. [1660].

[97] **Doncker, Hendrick**, 1626-1699.

The sea-atlas or the watter-world, shewing all the sea-coasts of y known parts of y earth with a generall doscription [sic] of the same. Verie vsefull for all masters & mates of shipps & likwise for merchants newly sett forth.

At Amsterdam, by Henry Doncker, bockseller; in the Newbridge Street, in the Stiremans Ghereetschap. Anno 1660.

[98] **Blaeu, Joan**, 1596-1673.

Atlas maior, siue, Cosmographia Blauiana, qua solum, salum, coelum, accuratissime describuntur.

Amstelaedami, labore & sumptibus Ioannis Blaeu, MDCLXII. [1662].

[99] *Kort verhael van Nieuw-Nederlants gelegentheit, deughden, natuerlijcke voorrechten, en byzondere bequaemheidt ter bevolkingh mitsgaders eenige requesten, vertoogen, deductien, enz. ten dien einden door eenige liefhebbers ten verscheide tijden omtrent 't laetst van 't jaer 1661. gepresenteert aen de A.A. Heeren Burgermeesteren dezer stede, of derzelver E.E. Heeren Gecommitteerde, enz. Ziet breeder achter de voor-reden den korten inhout, mitsgaders de waerschouwingh aen de boek-verkoopers staende hier vervolgens op d'ander-of tegen-zijde.*

[Amsterdam?] Gedrukt in 't jaer 1662.

[100] **Brugge, Jacob Segersz van der**, fl. 1634.

Journael, of dagh-register, gehouden by seven matroosen in haer overwinteren op Spitsbergen in Maurits-Bay, gelegen in Groenlandt, t'zedert het vertreck van de visscherey-schepen der Geoctroyeerde Noordtsche Compagnie, in Nederlandt, zijnde den 30. augusty, 1633. tot de wederkomst der voorsz. schepen, den 27. may anno 1634. Beschreven door den bevelhebber Jacob Sergersz. van der Brugge.

t' Amsterdam, gedruckt by Gillis Joosten Saeghman, in de Nieuwe-straet, ordinaris drucker van de journalen der zee-en landt-reysen. [1663?].

[101] **La Peyrère, Isaac de**, 1594-1676.

Drie voyagien gedaen na Groenlandt, om te ondersoecken of men door de Nauewte Hudsons soude konnen seylen; om alsoo en doorvaert te vinden. Alle ten versoecke van Christianus de IIII. koningh van Denemarcken, &c. de eerste door Ioan Monnick, de tweede door Marten Forbisser, ende de derde door Gotske Lindenau. Als mede een beschryvinghe, hoe, en op wat Wijse men de waluisschen vanght. Item, een korte beschryvingh van Groenlandt, met de manieren en hoedanicheden inwoonderen aldaer.

t' Amsterdam, gedruckt by Gillis Joosten Saeghman, in de Nieuwe-straet, ordinaris drucker van de journalen der zee-en landt-reysen. [1663?].

[102] Potgieter, Barent Jansz, b. 1574.

Journael van 't geene vijf schepen, van Rotterdam, in't jaer 1598. den 27. juny, na de Straet Magalanes varende, over gekomen is, tot den 21. january 1600. toe, op welcken dagh Capiteyn Sebald de Weert, met het schip 't Geloove genaemt, de selve straet verlatende, gedwonghen wiert weder naer huys te keeren: mitsgaders hoe de voorsz. capiteyn, niet sonder groot perijckel uyt gestaen te hebben, den 13 July, desselven jaers 1600. tot Rotterdam weder aan gekomen is. Verhalende veel wonderlijcke saecken die zy gesien hebben. ...

t' Amsterdam, gedruckt by Gillis Joosten Saeghman, in de Nieuwe-straet, ordinaris drucker, van de journalen ter zee, en de landt-reysen. [1663?].

[103] *Zeekere vrye-voorslagen, en versoeken, tot bevorderingh van een bestandige, voor Hollandt hooghnutte, en niet min verheerlijkende vrye volx uitzetting, tot verbreiding, of voort-planting van des zelfs vryen staet, in 't ongemeen gezont van climaet, en zeer vruchtbaar, mitsgaders rivieren vische-rijck Nieuw-Nederlandt. Als meede een by-gevoeght beknopt verhael van des zelve Nieuw-Nederlants gelegentheit ... Het eerste deel.*

t' Amsterdam, gedruck voor den autheur, en men vindtze te koop by Jan Rieuwertsz. in Dirk-van-Assen-en by Pieter Arentsz. inde Beurs-steeg., 1663.

[104] *A discription of the Coleny of Surranam in Guiana drawne in the yeare 1667.*

[Surinam, 1667].

[105] Witt, Johan de, 1625-1672.

A discourse by Mr. De Witt concerning Surynam.

[England, 1669 [i.e. 1719?]]

[106] Montanus, Arnoldus, 1625?-1683.

De Nieuwe en onbekende Weereld: of Beschryving van America en 't Zuid-Land, vervaetende d'oorsprong der Americænen en Zuid-Landers, gedenkwaardige togte derwaerds, gelegendheid der vaste kusten, eilanden, steden, sterkten, dorpen, tempels, bergen, fonteinen, stroomen, huisen, de natuur van beesten, boomen, planten en vreemde gewasschen, gods-dienst en zeden, wonderlijke voorvallen, vereeuwde en nieuwe oorloogen: verciert met af-beeldsels na 't leven in America gemaekt, en beschreeven door Arnoldus Montanus.

t' Amsterdam, by Jacob Meurs boek-verkooper en plaet-snyder, op de Kaisars-graft, schuin over de Wester-markt, in de stad Meurs. Anno 1671.

[107] *Omstandigh verhael van de Fransche rodomontade voor het Fort Curassou.*

[Amsterdam? 1673].

[108] Freire, Francisco de Brito.

Nova Lusitania, historia da guerra brasilica a purissima alma e savdosa memoria do serenissimo principe dom Theodosio principe de Portugal, e principe do Brasil. Por Francisco de Brito Freyre. Decada primeira.

Lisboa na officina de Joam Galram. Anno 1675.

[109] Goos, Pieter, ca. 1616-1675.

De zee-atlas, ofte water-wereld, waer in vertoont werden alle de zee-kusten van het bekende des aerd-bodems. Seer dienstigh voor alle heeren en kooplieden, als oock voor alle schippers en stuurlieden.

Gesneden, gedruckt en uytgegeven t'Amsteldam, by de weduwe van Pieter Goos, in de Zee-Spiegel, 1675.

[110] *A new draught of Surranam upon the coast of Guianna made and sold by John Thornton Hydrographer at the signe of England Scotland and Ireland in the Minories.*

London, John Thornton, [ca. 1675].

[111] Holland (Netherlands : Province). Staten.

Een vertoogh van de considerabele colonie, by de Edele Groot Mog. Heeren Staten van Hollandt ende West-Vrieslandt, uytgeset op de vaste kust van America. 1. De favorabele con-ditien, by haer Edele Groot Mog. vergunt aen hondert per-soonen, die haer eerst als principalen in de associatie sullen inlaten. 2. Een onderrichtinge van de goede gelegentheden van die landen, met de voordeelen, profiten en winsten die men aldaer na de conditien ende encouragementen by haer Edele Groot Mog. toegestaen, met een geringh capitael in weynige jaren doen kan, met een aenwysinge van de wyse en maniere van't cultiveren van de principaelste vruchten en waren. 3. Met een korte oplossinge van de swarigheden by eenige voorgewent.

In 's Graven-Hage, by Jacobus Scheltus, ordinaris drucker van de Edele Groot Mog. Heeren Staten van Hollandt ende West-Vrieslandt, woonende op't Binnen-Hoff, Anno 1676.

[112] *Pertinente beschrijvinge van Guiana. Gelegen aen de vaste kust van America. Waer in kortelijck verhaelt wordt, het aenmerckelijckste dat in en omtrent het landt van Guiana valt, als de limiten, het klimaet en de stoffen der landen, de mineralen, edele gesteenten, vruchten dieren, ende over-vloedigheyt der vissen, nevens der selver inwoonderen aldaer. Hier is bygevoeght der participanten uytschot ende profijten, die daer uytte volgen staen. Als oock de condtien van mijn heeren de staten van Hollandt en West-Vrieslandt, voor die gene die nae Guiana begeeren te varen.*

t'Amsterdam. By Jan Claesz. ten Hoorn, boeckverkoper tegen over 't Oude Heeren Logement. 1676.

[113] Exquemelin, A. O. (Alexandre Olivier).

De Americaensche zee-roovers. Behelsende een pertinente en waerachtige beschrijving van alle de voornaemste roveryen, en onmenschelijcke wreedheden, die de Engelse en Franse rovers, tegens de Spanjaerden in America, gepleeght hebben. Verdeelt in drie deelen: het eerste deel verhandelt hoe de Fransen op Hispanjola gekomen zijn, de aerdt van't landt, inwoonders, en hun manier van leven aldaer. Het tweede deel, de opkomst van de rovers, hun regel en leven onder malkander, nevens verscheyde roveryen aen de Spanjaerden gepleeght. Het derde 't verbranden van de stadt Panama, door d'Engelsche en Franse rovers gedaen, nevens het geen de schrijver op sijn reys voorgevallen is. Hier achter is bygevoeght, een korte verhandel-ing van de macht en rijkdommen, die de Koninck van Spanje,

Karel de Tweede, in America heeft, nevens des selfs inkomsten en regering aldaer. Als mede een kort begrijp van alle de voornaemste plaetsen in het selve gewest, onder Christen potentaten behoorende. Beschreven voor A. O. Exquemelin. Die self alle dese roveryen, door noodt, bygewoont heeft. Met schoone figuren, kaerten, en conterfeytsels, alle na 't leven geteeckent, versien.

t'Amsterdam. By Jan ten Hoorn, boeckverkoper, over 't Oude Heeren Logement. Anno 1678.

[114] **Ryder, Robert**.

Long Iland Siruaide by Robartte Ryder.
[New York? 1679?]

[115] *Eduward Meltons, Engelsch edelmans, zeldzaame en gedenkwaardige zee-en land-reizen; door Egypten, West-Indien, Perzien, Turkyen, Oost-Indien, en d'aangrenzende gewesten; behelzende een zeer naauwkeurige beschrijving der genoemde landen, benevens der zelver inwoonderen godsdienst, regeering, zeden en gewoonten, mitsgaders veele zeer vreemde voorvallen, ongemeene geschiedenissen, en wonderlijke wedervaringen. Aangevangen in den jaare 1660. en geëindigd in den jaare 1677. Vertaald uit d'eigene anteekeningen en brieven van den gedagten Heer Melton; en met verscheidene schoone kopere figuuren versierd.*

't Amsterdam, by Jan ten Hoorn, boek-verkooper over 't Oude Heeren-Logement, Anno 1681.

[116] **Neyn, Pieter de**, b. 1643.

Lust-hof der huwelyken, behelsende verscheyde seldsame ceremonien en plechtigheden, die voor desen by verscheyde natien en volckeren soo in Asia, Europa, Africa als America in gebruyck zyn geweest, als wel die voor meerendeel noch hedendaegs gebruykt ende onderhouden werden. Naeuw-keurigh, soo uyt oude als nieuwe schryvers by een vergaders door P. de Neyn .... Mitgaders desselfs Vrolycke uyren, uyt verscheyde soorten van mengel-dichten bestaande.

't Amsterdam, by Jan Bouman, boeckverkooper inde Kalverstraet, 1681.

[117] **Nieuhof, Johannes**, 1618-1672.

Johan Nieuhofs Gedenkweerdige Brasiliaense zee- en lant-reize. Behelzende al het geen op dezelve is voorgevallen. Beneffens een bondige beschrijving van gantsche Neerlants Brasil, zoo van lantschappen, steden, dieren, gewassen, als draghten, zeden en godsdienst der inwoonders: en inzonderheit een wijtloopig verhael der merkwaardigste voorvallen en geschiedenissen, die zich, geduurende zijn negenjarigh verblijf in Brasil, in d'oorlogen en opstant der Portugesen tegen d'onzen, zich sedert het jaer 1640. tot 1649. hebben toegedragen. Doorgaens verçiert met verscheide afbeeldingen, na 't leven aldaer getekent.

t'Amsterdam, voor de weduwe van Jacob van Meurs, op de Keizers-gracht. 1682.

[118] **Vries, Simon de**, b. 1630.

Curieuse aenmerckingen der bysonderste Oost en West-Indische verwonderens-waerdige dingen; nevens die van China, Africa, en andere gewesten des werelds. Bevattende 't voornaemste van alles, wat oyt nauwkeurighs en seldsaems van deese landen, ten opsight van der selver gelegenheyd; gestalte der aerde, berghwercken, gewassen, zeeën, rivieren; seeden en Godsdiensten der menschen, &c. Is ondervonden en opgeteeckend van een seer groote meenighte der geloofwaerdighste ooghgetuygen onder meest al de natien in Europa. En uyt deselve in een bequaeme

orde gebraght; oock soo met ondersoeckende als vergelijckende redenvoeringen verhandelt, door S. de Vries. In IV. deelen.

t'Utrecht, by Johannes Ribbius, boeckverkooper in de korte Jans-straet, M.DC.LXXXII. [1682].

[119] **Visscher, Nicolaes**, 1618-1679.

Novi Belgii Novaeque Angliae nec non partis partis Virginiae tabula multis in locis emendata per Nicolaum Visscher.

[Amsterdam, ca. 1682].

[120] **Wit, Frederik de**, 1630-1706.

Caerte van de rivieren van Suriname en Commowine met der selver uytstroomende creecken, met alle de landen soo verre de selve bewoonde worden.

[Amsterdam, Frederik de Wit, 1688].

[121] **United Provinces of the Netherlands. Staten Generaal**.

Copia van 't octroy door de Hoogh Mog. Heeren Staten Generael der Vereenighde Nederlanden, gegeven aan Jan Reeps, en syne mede participanten, om een colonie op te rechten aen de westzyde van Rio de las Amasones, tot aen Cabo d'Orange. Mitgaders een korte beschryvinge van de landen, vruchten gedierten, ende visschen, &c. nevens eenige opgestelde condition, om een compagnie te maecken, tot voortsettinge van dese colonie, ten meesten voordeele van de gemene participanten.

In 's Graven-hage, by Jacobus Scheltus, ordinaris drucker van de Hoogh Mogende Heeren Staten Generael der Vereenighde Nederlanden. Anno 1689.

[122] *Pertinent en waarachtig verhaal van alle de handelingen en directie van Pedro van Belle, ontrent den slavenhandel, ofte, het Assiento de Negros, eerst door D. Juan Barosso y Posso, bij zijn overlijden door D. Nicolas Porsio, en daar na door Balthasar Coijmans met den Koning van Spangien aangegaan, zoo in Spangien, de West-Indijes, als op Curaçao: dienende tot onderrichtinge van alle die gene, die bij het voorsz. Assiento, ofte de Compagnie van Coijmans en Van Belle tot Cadix, eenigsints zouden mogen wezen geinteresseert.*

Te Rotterdam, bij Reinier Leers, MDCLXXXIX. [1689].

[123] **Sterre, Dionysius van der**, d. 1691.

Zeer aanmerkelijke reysen gedaan door Jan Erasmus Reining, meest in de West-Indien en ook in veel andere deelen des werelds. &c. Waer in kortelijk verhandelt werd het geen hem van syn kintsche jaren avontuurlyk ter zee en te land tot zijn 49ste jaar is voorgevallen, soo tegens de wilden, als voor en tegens de Spanjaarden, en voor en tegens de Engelschen, Franse, Portugese en meer andere natien: groote hongers-nood, schrikkelijke elende, perijkelen zijns levens, stoute actien, kloekmoedige uitvoeringen, en victorieuse verrigtinge; samengesteld door D. vander Sterre, med. doct. op Curacao. Met figuren.

t'Amsterdam, by Jan ten Hoorn, boekverkooper over 't Oude Heere Logement in den History-Schryver. 1691.

[124] **Berkel, Adriaan van**.

Amerikaansche voyagien, behelzende een reis na Rio de Berbice, gelegen op het vaste land van Guiana, aande wildekust van America, mitsgaders een andere na de colonie van Suriname, gelegen in het noorder deel van het gemelde landschap Guiana. Ondermengd met alle de byzonderheden noopende de zeden, gewoonten, en levenswijs der inboorlingen, boom-en aardgewassen, waaren en koopmanschappen, en andere aanmerkelijke zaaken. Beschreven door Adriaan van

Berkel. Vercierd met kopere plaaten.

Tot Amsterdam, by Johan ten Hoorn, boekverkooper tegen over het Oude Heeren Logement, inde Historischryver, 1695.

[125] **Graaff, Nicolaus de**, ca. 1617-ca. 1701.

Reisen van Nicolaus de Graaff, na de vier gedeeltens des werelds, als Asia, Africa, America en Europa. Behelsende een beschryving van sijn 48 jarige reise en aanmerkelykste voorvallen, die hy heeft gesien en die hem zyn ontmoet. Van de levenswyse der volkeren, Godsdienst, regeringe, landschappen en steden. Als ook een nette, dog korte beschryving van China, desselfs over groote landschappen, menigvuldige steden, gebouwen, gegraven kanalen, scheepvaard, outheid der Chinesen: mitsgaders derselver oorlogen tegen de Tartaren; en op wat wyse de Tartar sig meester van China heeft gemaakt. Hier agter is by gevoegd d'Oost-Indise spiegel, zynde een beschryving van deselve schryver van geheel Oost-Indiën, de levenswyse so der Hollanders in Indiën, als op de schepen, en een net verhaal van de uit en t'huis reise. Met curieuse koperen platen verçiert.

Tot Hoorn, gedrukt by Feyken Ryp, boekdrukker over 't Stadhuis. En zyn mede te bekomen tot Amsterdam by Hendrik en de Wed: Dirk Boom. Uitregt by Antoni Schouten. Anno 1701.

[126] **Bosman, Willem**.

Nauwkeurige beschryving van de Guinese Goud- Tand- en Slave-kust, nevens alle desselfs landen, koningryken, en gemenebesten, van de zeeden der inwoonders, hun godsdienst, regeering, regtspleeging, oorlogen, trouwen, begraven, enz. Mitsgaders de gesteltheid des lands, veld-en boomgewassen, alderhande dieren, zo wilde als tamme, viervoetige en kruipende, als ook 't pluim-gedierte, vissen en andere zeldzaamheden meer, tot nogtoe de Europeërs onbekend; door Willem Bosman....

t'Utrecht, by Anthony Schouten, boekverkoper in de Korte Jans-straat. 1704.

[127] *Naaukeurige versameling der gedenk-waardigste zee en land-reysen na Oost en West-Indiën, mitsgaders andere gewesten, ter eerster ontdekking en soo vervolgens van verscheyde volkeren, meerendeels door vorsten, of maatschappyen derwaarts gefonden, gedaan; waar van eenige noyt gedrukt, andere nu eerst uyt haar oorspronkelijke taalen overgeset, en sommige merkelijk verbeterd zijn; beginnende met het jaar 1246. en eyndigende op dese tijd ....*

In het ligt gegeven te Leyden, door Pieter vander Aa, boekverkoper in de St. Pieters Koor-steeg, in Plato. 1707.

[128] **Martens, Friedrich**, 1635-1699.

Frederik Martens nauwkeurige beschryvinge van Groenland of Spitsbergen, waer in de walvisch-vangst, gelegentheyd van 't ys, en haer wonderlijke kragt en figuren, duydelijk word aengewesen: nevens den aard van 't land, gewassen, ys-bergen, gevogelte, viervoetige dieren, en visschen deser contreyen. Oock hoe de walvisschen gevangen, gekapt en gesneden worden: benevens verscheyde avontuurlijke voorvallen in Groenland. Met een verhaal van de gevange walvisch by St. Anne-Land. Als mede de walvisch-vangst op rym. Met kopere platen verçiert.

Tot Amsterdam, by de wed: van Gysbert de Groot, boekverkoopster op de Nieuwe-dijk in de Groote Bybel. 1710.

[129] **Arents Bergh** (ship)

[Journal of an officer on the Dutch merchant ship Arents Bergh *of Amsterdam on her voyage from Amsterdam to Curaçao and the Spanish Main, 1714-1715].*

[On board the *Arents Bergh*, in Atlantic and Caribbean waters, 21 April 1714-23 March 1715?].

[130] **Herlein, J. D.**

Beschryvinge van de volk-plantinge Zuriname: vertonende de opkomst dier zelver colonie, de aanbouw en bewerkinge der zuiker-plantagien. Neffens den aard der eigene natuurlijke inwoonders of indianen; als ook de slaafsche Afrikaansche Mooren; deze beide natien haar levens-manieren, afgoden-dienst, regering, zeden, gewoonten en dagelijksche bezigheden. Mitsgaders een vertoog van de bosch-grond, water-en pluim-gediertens; de veel vuldige heerlijke vrugten, melk-agtige zappen, gommen, olyen, en de gehele gesteltheid van de Karaïbaansche kust. Door J.D. Hl. Verrijkt met de land-kaart (daar de legginge der plantagien worden aangewezen) en kopere platen.

Te Leeuwarden, by Meindert Injema, boek-drukker en verkoper voor aan in de St. Jakobs-straat, 1718.

[131] *Totius Neobelgii nova et accuratissima tabula.*

Typus Ioachim Ottens Amstelodami [ca. 1718].

[132] **Merian, Maria Sibylla**, 1647-1717.

Mariæ Sibillæ Merian Dissertatio de generatione et metamorphosibus insectorum Surinamensium in qua[m], præter vermes et erucas Surinamenses, earumque admirandam metamorphosin, plantæ, flores & fructus, quibus vescuntur, & quibus fuerunt inventæ, exhibentur. His adiunguntur bufones, lacerti, serpentes, araneæ, aliaque admiranda istius regionis animalcula; omnia manu ejusdem matronæ in America ad vivum accurate depicta, & nunc æri incisa. Accedit appendix transformationum piscium in ranas, & ranarum in pisces.

Amstelædami, apud Joannem Oosterwyk, MDCCXIX. [1719].

[133] **Zorgdrager, C.G.** (Cornelis Gijsbertz), b. ca. 1650.

C:G: Zorgdragers bloeyende opkomst der aloude en hedendaagsche Groenlandsche visschery. Waar in met eene geoeffende ervaarenheit de geheele omslag deezer visscherye beschreeven, en wat daar in dient waargenomen, naaukeurig verhandelt wordt. Uitgebreid met eene korte historische beschryving der noordere gewesten, voornamentlyk Groenlandt, Yslandt, Spitsbergen, Nova Zembla, Jan Mayen Eilandt, de Straat Davis, en al 't aanmerklykste in d'ontdekking deezer landen, en in de visschery voorgevallen. Met byvoeging van de walvischvangst, in haare hoedanigheden, behandelingen, 't scheepsleeven en gedrag beschouwt. Door Abraham Moubach. Verciert met naaukeurige, correct en naar 't leven geteekende nieuwe kaarten en kunstige printverheelingen.

t'Amsterdam. By Johannes Oosterwyk, boekverkooper op den Dam, 1720.

[134] *Beschryving van de rivier en colonie der Barbice, geleegen aan de wilde kust van Gujana, bewesten van Suriname.*

Te Amsteldam, By Gerard van Keulen, boek-en zeekaart-verkooper, aan de oost-zyde van de Nieuwen-brug, op de hoek van de Nieuwenbrug-steeg. [1725?].

[135] **Van Santvoord, Cornelius**, 1686-1752.

Samenspraak over de Klaghte der Raritanders; so in 't gemeen, als wel in 't besonder, wegens het gene in die ter neder gestelt is ten laste van Cornelius Van Santvoord, Predikant op Staten-Eiland. Met een naschrift tot vrede.

Te Nieuw-York, gedrukt by J. Peter Zenger, 1726.

[136] **J. C. P. (Johann Christoph Praetorius).**

Tobago insulæ caraibicæ in America sitæ fatum. Seu, brevis & succinta insulæ huius descriptio . . . á J. C. P.

Groningæ, apud Jacobum Sipkes, MDCCXXVII. [1727].

[137] **Sikkena, Jan**, fl. 1727.

Nieuwe groote en seer curieuse paskaart van geheel-Westindien, vertoonende alle desselfs eylanden bayen en rivieren mitsgaders alle droogtens en dieptens, nieuwelyks en seer namen goede afpylingen en opservatien. Door Ian Sikkena leermeester der wiskonst met privilegie.

Tot Amsterdam by Gerard van Keulen boek en zeekaart verkooper aen de Nieuwen Brug [ca. 1727].

[138] **Real Compañía Guipuzcoana de Caracas.**

Manifiesto, que con incontestables hechos prueba los grandes beneficios, que ha producido el establecimiento de la Real Compañia Guipuzcoana de Caracas, y califica quan importante es su conservacion al estado, à la Real Hacienda, al bien publico, y à los verdaderos interesses de la misma provincia de Caracas.

[Madrid? 1749?].

[139] *Totius Neobelgii nova et accuratissima tabula.*

Apud Reinier & Iosua Ottens Amstelodami [between 1726 and 1750].

[140] **Lavaux, A. de**.

Algemeene kaart van de colonie of provintie van Suriname, met de rivieren, districten, ontdekkingen door militaire togten, en de grootte der gemeeten plantagien; door last, op kisten, en met approbatie der E. E. Heeren Directeurs van de Societeit, naar de naaukeurigste waarneemingen, door den ingenieur Alexander de Lavaux geteekend.

Te Amsterdam, by Cóvens en Mortier, met octroy van de Ed: Gr: Acht Heeren der Stadt Amsterdam [after 1758].

[141] *Kortbondige beschryvinge van de colonie de Berbice. Behelzende de legging, bevolking, uitgestrektheid, kreeken, forten, plantagien, enz. dezer colonie. De oorspronk, gods-dienst en zeden der Americaansche bewooners aldaar, hunne huwelyken, zeldzaame kraamhoudinge, opvoeding der kinderen, bezigheden, spyzen, dranken, hutten, ziektens, wapenen en zeldzaame wyze van begravingen. Vervolgens een beschryving van de negers of slaven, mitsgaders de staat der Europeaanen, die zig aldaar voorheen bevonden, en, verder een beschryving van de voornaamste producten welke deeze colonie voortbrengt. Verrykt met merkwaardige berichten wegens de onlangs onstaane en nog aanhoudende opstandt door de negers, en de gesteldheid aldaar, verzeldt met eenige bedenkelykheden om de colonie weder in vollen rust te herstellen, en de middelen om ze in 't vervolg daar voor te beveiligen. Uit de aanteekeningen van een voornaam heer opgemaakt, die eenige jaaren op de colonie zyn verblyf gehouden heeft. Opgeheldert met een kaart van de colonie de Berbice, en een plaat verbeeldende de wyze hoe de Indiaanen hun brood bakken, en de ceremonie hunner begraffenissen.*

Te Amsteldam, by S. K. Baalde boekverkoper op den Dam. MDCCLXIII. [1763].

[142] **Weilburgh Plantation, Rio Demerara**.

[Accounts ledger].

[Rio Demerara, ca. 1767-ca. June 1770; Kelso (?) Scotland, ca. Feb. 1786-ca. July 1787].

[143] **Hartsinck, Jan Jakob**, 1716-1779.

Beschryving van Guiana, of de wildekust in Zuid-America, betreffende de aardrykskunde en historie des lands, de zeeden en gewoontes der inwooners, de dieren, vogels, visschen, boomen en gewassen, als mede de eerste ontdekking dier kust, de bezittingen der Spanjaarden, Franschen en Portugeezen en voornaamelyk de volkplantingen der Nederlanderen, als Essequebo, Demerary, Berbice, Suriname, en derzelver rivieren, met de noodige kaarten en afbeeldingen der forten. Waarby komt eene verhandeling over den aart en de gewoontes der neger-slaaven. Alles uit echte stukken opgesteld door Mr. Jan Jacob Hartsinck, charter-en request-meester van het Edel Mogende Collegie ter Admiraliteit tot Amsterdam, mitsgaders lid van het Zeeuwsche Genootschap der Wetenschappen te Vlissingen.

Te Amsterdam, by Gerrit Tielenburg, MDCCLXX. [1770].

[144] **Fermin, Philippe**, 1729-1813.

Nieuwe algemeene beschryving van de colonie van Suriname. Behelzende al het merkwaardige van dezelve, met betrekkinge tot de historie, aardryks-en natuurkunde. Door Philip Fermin, M.D.

Te Harlingen, ter drukkerye van V. van der Plaats Junior. MDCCLXX. [1770].

[145] **Winter, Nicolaas Simon van**, 1718-1795.

Monzongo, of De koningklyke slaaf. Treurspel. Door Nicolaas Simon Van Winter.

Te Amsterdam, by Pieter Meijer, op den Dam. 1774.

[146] **New York (State). Committee of Safety**.

To the inhabitants of the colony of New-York. To prevent, as much as possible, the evil consequences which may arise from the assertion, that the "Continental Congress have made no approaches towards an accommodation with Great-Britain," the Committee of Safety of the colony of New-York, have directed the following Petition of the Continental Congress, to His Majesty; and the address of the Lord Mayor and Livery of London, to the electors of Great-Britain, occasioned by that Petition; to be published.

New York: printed by John Holt, near the Coffee-House. [1776].

[147] **Romans, Bernard, ca.** 1720-ca. 1784.

Annals of the troubles in the Netherlands. From the accession of Charles V. Emperor of Germany. In four parts. A proper and seasonable mirror for the present Americans. Collected and translated from the most approved historians in the native tongue. By Bernard Romans.

Hartford: printed by Watson and Goodwin, for the author. M.DCC.LXXVIII-M,DCC,LXXXII. [1778-1782].

[148] **Hering, Johannes Hermanus**, 1731-1790?

Beschryving van het eiland Curaçao, en de daar onder hoorende eilanden, Bon-Aire, Oroba en Klein Curaçao. Benevens een kort bericht, wegens het gesprongen schip Alphen, door J.H. Hering.

Te Amsterdam, by Joannes van Selm, MDCCLXXIX. [1779].

[149] *Missive van bewindhebberen der Westindische Compagnie, met een deductie door den commandeur van St. Eustatius, J. de Graaf, aan hun overgegeven, soo ten opsigte van de klagten door het Hof van Engeland tegens hem ingebragt, als het geen geduurende sijn commando op voorschreeve eyland is verrigt. Det. 23 Maart, 1779. Rec. 31 Maart, 1779.*

[Amsterdam?] 1779.

[150] **Cramer, Peter**, 1726-1782.

De uitlandsche kapellen voorkomende in de drie waereld-deelen Asia, Africa en America, by een verzameld en beschreeven door den Heer Pieter Cramer, directeur van het Zeeuwsch Genootschap te Vlissingen, lid van het Genootschap Concordia et Libertate te Amsteldam. Onder deszelfs opzigt allen naar het leven getekend, in het koper gebragt en met natuurlyke koleuren afgetekend. Papillons exotiques des trois parties de monde l'Asie, l'Afrique et l'Amerique. Rassemblés et décrits par Mr. Pierre Cramer, Directeur de la Societe Zelandoise des Sciences a Vlissingue et membre de la Societe Concordia et Libertate a Amsteldam. Dessines sur les originaux, gravés et enluminés sous sa direction.

A Amsteldam, chez S. J. Baalde. A Utrecht, chez Barthelemy Wild. MDCCLXXIX-MDCCLXXXII. [1779-1782].

[151] **Surinam**.

Reglement. Of Ordre waarna een ieder colonier en ingezeeten dezer colonie Surinamen in cas van alarm weegens buitenlandsche vyanden zig stiptelyk zullen hebben te gedragen.

[Paramaribo] Herdrukt ter geprivilegeerde drukkery van A.T. Bordas te Paramaribo. [1807].

[152] **Van der Kemp, Francis Adrian**, 1752-1829

Verzameling van stukken tot de dertien Vereenigde Staeten van Noord-America betrekkelijk.

Te Leyden, bij L. Herdingh, MDCCLXXXI. [1781].

[153] *Lierzang op de verklaarde onafhanglijkheid der Noord-Amerikaansche Staeten.*

[Dordrecht, 1782].

[154] **Adams, John**, 1735-1826.

Geschiedenis van het geschil tusschen Groot-Britannie en Amerika, zedert deszelfs oorsprong, in den jaare 1754, tot op den tegenwoordigen tijd. Door zijn excellentie, den heere John Adams, Schildknaap, gevolmagtigden staatsdienaar der dertien Vereenigde Staaten van Noord-Amerika, bij de Republijk der Vereenigde Nederlanden..

Te Amsteldam: bij W. Holtrop, 1782.

[155] **Roos, Paul François,** ca. 1750-1805.

Eerstelingen van Surinaamsche mengelpoëzy, door P.F. Roos.

Te Amsteldam, by Hendrik Gartman. MDCCLXXXIII. [1783].

[156] **Nomsz, Johannes**, 1738-1803.

Cora, of de Peruanen, treurspel. Door J. Nomsz.

Te Amsteldam, by de erven van David Klippink. MDCCLXXXIV. [1784].

[157] **Nomsz, Johannes**, 1738-1803.

Bartholomeus Las Casas, treurspel. Door J. Nomsz.

Te Amsteldam, by Willem Holtrop, MDCCLXXXV. [1785].

[158] **Blom, Anthony**, d. 1808.

Verhandeling van den landbouw, in de colonie Suriname, door Anthony Blom.

Te Amsteldam, bij J.W. Smit, boek-en konstverkooper. MDCCLXXXVII. [1787].

[159] **Bourgeois, Nicolas Louis**, 1710?-1776?

Voyages intéressans dans différentes colonies françaises, espagnoles, anglaises, &c; contenants des observations importantes relatives à ces contrées; & un mémoire sur les maladies les plus communes à Saint-Domingue, leurs remèdes, & le moyen de s'en préserver moralement & phisiquement: avec des anecdotes singulières, qui n'avaient jamais été publiées. Le tout rédigé & mis au jour, d'après un grand nombre de manuscrits, par M. N. ...

A Londres et se trouve à Paris, chez Jean-François Bastien. M.DCC.LXXXVIII. [1788].

[160] *Essai historique sur la colonie de Surinam, sa fondation, ses révolutions, ses progrès, depuis son origine jusqu'à nos jours, ainsi que les causes qui depuis quelques années ont arreté le cours de sa prosperité; avec la description & l'état actuel de la colonie, de même que ses révenus annuels, les charges & impots qu'on y paye, comme aussi plusieurs autres objets civils & politiques; ainsi qu'un tableau des moeurs de ses habitans en général. Avec l'histoire de la nation juive portugaise & allemande y etablie, leurs privilêges immunités & franchises: leur etat politique & moral, tant ancien que moderne: la part qu'ils ont eu dans la défense & dans les progrès de la colonie. Le tout redigé sur des pieces authentiques y jointes, & mis en ordre par les régens & réprésentans de ladite nation juive Portugaise.*

A Paramaribo, 1788.

[161] *Raport aan Zijne Doorluchtigste Hoogheid den Heere Prince van Orange en Nassau &&& overgegeven van wegen Hoogst des Zelfs Commissarissen naar de colonien van den staat in de West Indien betreffende het eiland Curacao.*

[Curaçao? c. 1790].

[162] **Schoute, H.**

Gezicht van het West-Indisch-Huys, op de binnenplaats te zien, tot Amsterdam. Vue de la Maison de la Compagnie des Indes Occidentales, à Amsterdam.

Te Amsterdam by P. Fouquet junior. à Amsterdam chez P. Fouquet junior. [ca. 1790].

[163] *Weeklyksche Surinaamsche Courant.*

Gedrukt te Paramaribo by W.W. Beeldsnyder, ter gepriviligeerde drukkery der Edele Directie en 't Land, 4 July 1793-26 Juny 1794.

[164] **Stedman, John Gabriel**, 1744-1797.

Narrative, of a five years' expedition, against the revolted Negroes of Surinam, in Guiana, on the wild coast of South America: from the year 1772, to 1777: elucidating the history of that country, and the description of its productions, viz. quadrupedes, birds, fishes, reptiles, trees, shrubs, fruits, & roots; with an account of the indians of Guiana, & Negroes of Guinea. By Captn. J.G. Stedman. Illustrated with 80 elegant engravings, designed from nature, by the author.

London. Printed by J. Johnson, St. Pauls Church Yard, & J. Edwards, Pall Mall, 1796.

[165] **Bouchenroeder, Friedrich**, Freiherr von.

Carte generale, & particuliere de la colonie d'Essequebe, & Demerarie située dans la Guiane, en Amérique redigée & dediée au Comité des Colonies & Possessions de la Republique Batave en Amérique, & a la côte du Guinée. Par le major F. Von Bouchenroeder. 1798.

[166] **Van der Kemp, Francis Adrian**, 1752-1829.

Lofrede op George Washington, te Oldenbarneveld, den 22sten van Sprokkelmaand 1800, in Oneida district, staat van New York, in de Engelsche taale uitgesprooken, door Franc. Adr. van der Kemp.

Te Amsterdam, by Gerrit Warnars. MDCCC. [1800].

[167] **Vosmaer, A. (Arnout)**, 1720-1799.

Natuurkundige beschryving eener uitmuntende verzameling van zeldsaame gedierten, bestaande in Oost- en Westindische viervoetige dieren, vogelen en slangen, weleer leevend voorhanden geweest zynde, buiten den Haag, op het Kleine Loo van Z. D. H. den prins van Oranje-Nassau, door A. Vosmaer … met naar 't leven getekende en gecouleurde afbeeldingen.

Te Amsterdam, by J. B. Elwe, MDCCCIV. [1804].

[168] **Pinckard, George**, 1768-1835.

Notes on the West Indies: written during the expedition under the command of the late general Sir Ralph Abercromby: including observations on the island of Barbadoes, and the settlements captured by the British troops, upon the coast of Guiana; likewise remarks relating to the creoles and slaves of the western colonies, and the Indians of South America: with occasional hints, regarding the seasoning, or yellow fever of hot climates. By George Pinckard, M.D. of the Royal College of Physicians, Deputy Inspector-General of Hospitals to His Majesty's Forces, and physician to the Bloomsbury Dispensary. In three volumes.

London: printed for Longman, Hurst, Rees and Orme, Paternoster-Row. 1806.

[169] **Jong van Rodenburgh, Cornelius de**, 1762-1838.

Reize naar de Caribische eilanden, in de jaren 1780 en 1781; door Cornelius de Jong, toen ter als tijd luitenant dienende, aan boord van s'lands schip van oorlog Mars onder bevel van den schout bij nacht Willem Krul. Met platen.

Te Haarlem, bij François Bohn, MDCCCVII. [1807].

[170] *Kort historisch verhaal van den eersten aanleg, lotgevallen en voortgang der particuliere colonie Berbice gelegen in het landschap Guiana in Zuid-America; in het bijzonder behandelende het onderwerp der privaate eigendomme der Societeit van participanten in die colonie, en wel allerbijzonderst de zoogenaamde akkergelden. Met eene openlegging van het singulier en contrasteerend gedrag van den Heere Abraham Jacob van Imbyze van Batenburg, ale Civil Gouverneur der Colonie. Door een colonist in Augustus 1805. Met eene gekleurde afbeelding..*

Te Amsterdam, bij C. Sepp Jansz., MDCCCVII. [1807].

[171] **Oxholm, J.N.**

Bibel voor kinders of Bibels spreek met kort opmuntringen voor opmerksame kinders set over na die creols tael van J.N. Oxholm Deen dominie en missionarius in St. Crux en inspector over die Deen Westindis eilanden.

Kopenhamn, 1822.

[172] **Kuhn, F.A.**

Beschouwing van den toestand der Surinaamsche plantagieslaven. Eene oeconomisch-geneeskundige bijdrage tot verbetering deszelven. Door F. A. Kuhn, M. D. ridder der Orde van den Nederlandschen Leeuw, Chirn. en Chef Z.M. Troepen en Hospitalen te Surinamen mitsgaders Stads doctor en phijsicus aldaar.

Te Amsterdam, bij C. G. Sulpke. MDCCCXXVIII. [1828].

[173] **Voorduin, G.W.C.**

Gezigten uit Neerland's West-Indien, naar de natuur geteekend, en beschreven door G.W.C. Voorduin …

Amsterdam: F. Buffa, [1860-1862].

Addendum to the Chronological List

[A1] **Colom, Arnold**.

Pas caarte van Nieu Nederlandt uytgegeven door Arnold Colom.

t'Amsterdam opt Water by de Nieuwe brugh in de Lichtende Colom. [ca. 1656].

[A2] **Jansson, Jan, 1588-1664**.

Tabula Magellanica, qua Tierrae del Fuego. cum celeverrimis fretis a F. Magellano et I. Le Maire detectis novissima et accuratissima descriptio exhibetur.

Amstelodami, apud Joannem Janssonium. [ca. 1659?].

[A3] **West Indische Compagnie (Netherlands)**.

Remonstrantie, vande bewinthebberen der Nederlantsche West-Indische Compagnie, aende d'Heeren Staten Generael over verscheyde specien van tyrannye, ende gewelt, door de Engelsche in Nieuw-Nederlant, aende onderdanen van haer Hoogh-Mog: verrecht, en hoe sy reparatie, ende justitie versoecken.

Schidam, voor Pieter Sanders, Anno 1663.

[A4] *[Surinam and Commewijne Rivers. Manuscript map].* [Holland? 1667 or later].

[A5] *Caerte ofte vertooninge vande riuieren van Suriname en Comewijne met verscheyde creken uyt deselue spruijtende als Para Surinoo en Cotteca ende ander meer gelyck die nu tegen woordich bewoont verden.* [Amsterdam?] Anno 1671.

[A6] **Jollain**.

Nowel Amsterdam en Lamerique. 1672. [Amsterdam, ca. 1672].

[A7] **Bos, Lambert van den, 1610-1698**.

Leeven en daden der doorluchtighste zee-helden en ontdeckers van landen deser eeuwen. Beginnende met Christoffel Colombus, vinder van de nieuwe wereldt. En eyndigende met den roemruchtigen Admiraeel M.A. de Ruyter, Ridd. &c. vertoonende veel vreemde voorvallen, dappere verrichtingen, stoutmoedige bestieringen, en swaere zee-slagen, &c. naeukeurigh, uyt veele geloofwaerdige schriften, en authenijcke stucken, by een gebracht, en beschreven door V.D.B.

t'Amsterdam, by Jan Claesz. ten Hoorn, en Jan Bouman, Boeckverkoopers. Anno 1676.

[A8] **Roggeveen, Arent, d. 1679**.

Le premier tóme [i.e. tome] de la tourbe ardante, illuminant toute la region des Indes Occidentales, commençant depuis rio Amazones, jusqu'a la partie septentrionále [i.e. septentrionale] de Terra Nova. Décrit par Arent Roggeveen.

[*A* Amsterdam, taileé [i.e. tailée], imprimé. & mis en lumiere par Pierre Goos, en compagnie de l'autheur. 1676.

[A9] **Hooghe, Romeyn de, 1645-1708**.

Afbeeldingh der heete rescontre te water en te lant op het eylandt Tabago, tusschen den Fransen Admirael d'Estrée, en den Heer Commandeur Binckes; in de maenden von February en Maert 1677 ... Opgedragen aen d'Ed: Moog: Heeren, mijne Heeren de Gecommitteerde Raden ter Admiraliteyt, resideerende binnen Amsterdam. Door haer onderdanige dienaer Romeyn de Hooge.

[Amsterdam, ca. 1677].

[A10] **Regters, Tiebaut, 1710-1768**.

Jan Nepveu, Gouverneur Generaal, van Suriname.

[Amsterdam], 1770.

[A11] *Den Britsen leopard tot reden gebracht.*

[Amsterdam, 1780].

[A12] **Colley, T., supposed engraver**.

The late auction at St Eustatia. By R___ & V___.

1781. Pub: by E. Hedges n 92 Cornhill. June 11, 1781.

[A13] *Lijkzang op het overlijden van 's lands glori, door Patriophilus.*

Te Amsterdam. [s.n., 1781].

[A14] **Gillray, James, 1757-1815**.

The Dutchman in the dumps.

[London], Pubd. April 9th. 1781, by W. Humphrey no 227 Strand, [1781].

[A15] **S., R**.

The ballance of power.

London. Published as ye Act directs, Jany 17. 1781. by R. Wilkinson, at No in Cornhill., [1781].

[A16] **Roos, Paul François, ca. 1750-1805**.

Surinaamsche mengelpoëzy, van P.F. Roos.

Te Amsteldam, by H. Gartman en P.J. Uylenbroek. MDCCCIV. [1804].

[A17] *Kort en bondig verhael, van 't geene in den oorlogh, tusschen den Koningh van Engelant &c. de H: M: Heeren Staten der vrye Vereenigde Nederlanden., en den bisschop van Munster is voorgevallen. Beginnende in den jare 1664. en eyndigende met het sluyten van de vrede tot Breda, in 't jaer 1667. Waer in de voornaemste geschiedenissen, in den selven oorlogh voorgevallen, beschreven worden. Met een korte inleydingh, vervattende de ballinghschap en herstelling van den tegenwoordigen Koningh van Engelandt. Met verscheyde kopere figuren verciert.*

't Amsterdam, voor Marcus Willemsz. Doornick, op den Vygendam, in 't Kantoor Incktvat. Anno 1667.

Alphabetical List of Works in the Catalogue

The boldface numerals refer to the Chronological List

Accoord van Brasilien. [**89**]

Acosta, José de. *Historie naturael ende morael.* [**6**]

Adams, John. *Geschiedenis van het geschil.* [**154**]

A discription of the Coleny of Surranam. [**104**]

Aenwysinge: datmen vande Oost en West-Indische Compagnien. [**64**]

Amsterdamsche veerman op Middelburgh. [**82**]

A new draught of Surranam. [**110**]

Arents Bergh. [**129**]

Augspurger, Johann Paul. *Kurtze und warhaffte Beschreibung.* [**65**]

Avontroot, Johannes. *Den grouwel der verwoestinghe.* [**29**]

Baardt, Pieter. *Petri Baardt Friesche Triton.* [**46**]

Baers, Johannes. *Olinda, ghelegen int Landt van Brasil.* [**47**]

Baerle, Caspar van. *Rerum per octennium in Brasilia.* [**71**]

Baerle, Caspar van. *Rerum per octennium in Brasilia.* [**96**]

Berkel, Adriaan van. *Amerikaansche voyagien.* [**124**]

Beschrijvinghe van Virginia. [**85**]

Beschryving van de rivier en colonie der Barbice. [**134**]

Blaeu, Joan. *Atlas major.* [**98**]

Blaeu, Willem Janszoon. *Tweede deel van 't Tooneel des aerdriicx.* [**51**]

Blom, Anthony. *Verhandeling van den landbouw.* [**158**]

Bos, Lambert van den. *Leeven en daden der doorluchtighste zee-helden.* [**A7**]

Bosman, Willem. *Nauwkeurige beschryving.* [**126**]

Bouchenroeder, Friedrich, Freiherr von. *Carte generale & particuliere.* [**165**]

Bourgeois, Nicolas Louis. *Voyages intéressans.* [**159**]

Brandt in Brasilien. [**76**]

Brasilsche gelt-Sack. [**73**]

Bril-gesicht voor de verblinde eyghen baetsuchtige handelaers op Brasil. [**54**]

Broeck, Matheus van den. *Journael, ofte historiaelse beschrijvinge.* [**84**]

Brouwer, Hendrick. *Journael ende historis verhael.* [**69**]

Brugge, Jacob Segersz van der. *Journael, of dagh-register.* [**100**]

Calado, Manuel. *O valeroso Lucideno.* [**77**]

Casas, Bartolomé de las. *Seer cort verhael.* [**3**]

Casas, Bartolomé de las. *Spieghel der Spaenscher tyrannye.* [**4**]

Casas, Bartolomé de las. *Spieghel der Spaenscher tyrannye.* [**10**]

Casas, Bartolomé de las. *Den spieghel der Spaense Tyrannye.* [**53**]

Colom, Arnold. *Pas caarte van Nieu Nederlandt.* [**A1**]

Caerte ofte voertooninge vande riuieren van Suriname. [**A5**]

Colley, T. *The late auction at St Eustatia.* [**A12**]

Consideratien vande vrede in Nederlandt. [**11**]

Corrêa, João de Medeiros. *Relaçam verdadeira.* [**35**]

Cort, bondigh ende waerachtigh verhael. [**90**]

Cramer, Peter. *De uitlandsche kapellen.* [**150**]

De Brasilsche breede-byl. [**72**]

Den Britsen leopard tot reden gebracht. [**A11**]

Den Nederlandtschen bye-corf. [**18**]

Dialogus oft tzamensprekinge, gemaect op den vrede-handel. [**12**]

Die Stat Olinda de Phernambuco. [**48**]

Discours by forme van remonstrantye. [**13**]

Discours op verscheyde voorslaghen. [**67**]

Donck, Adriaen van der. *Beschryvinge van Nieuvv-Nederlant.* [**91**]

Doncker, Hendrick. *The sea-atlas or the watter-world.* [**97**]

Eduward Meltons, Engelsch edelmans . . . zee- en land-reizen. [**115**]

Eenige advijsen ende verklaringhen uyt Brasilien. [**78**]

Eibergen, Rutgerus. *Svvymel-klacht.* [**41**]

Eroberung der reiche silber-vloot. [**42**]

Essai historique sur la colonie de Surinam. [**160**]

Exquemelin, Alexandre Olivier. *De Americaensche zee-roovers.* [**113**]

Fermin, Phillipe. *Nieuwe algemeene beschryving van de colonie van Suriname.* [**144**]

Freire, Francisco de Brito. *Nova Lusitania.* [**108**]

Gillray, James. *The Dutchman in the dumps.* [**A14**]

Goos, Pieter. *De zee-atlas, ofte water-wereld.* [**109**]

Graaff, Nicolaus de. *Reisen van Nicolaus de Graaff.* [**125**]

Grotius, Hugo. *Hugonis Grotii De origine gentium Americanarum.* [**62**]

Guelen, Auguste de. *Kort verhael Vanden staet van Fernanbuc.* [**60**]

Guerreiro, Bartolomeu. *Iornada dos vassalos da coroa de Portugal.* [**36**]

Hartsinck, Jan Jakob. *Beschryving van Guiana, of de wildekust.* [**143**]

Hering, J.H. *Beschryving van het eiland Curaçao.* [**148**]

Herlein, J.D. *Beschryvinge van de volk-plantinge Zuriname.* [**130**]

Holland, *Een vertoogh van de considerabele colonie.* [**111**]

't Hollandts rommelzootje. [**83**]

Hooghe, Romeyn de. *Afbeeldingh der heete rescontre te water.* [**A9**]

Iournael ofte kort discours, nopende de rebellye. [**68**]

Iournael vande Nassausche vloot. [**39**]

J.C.P. *Tobago insulae Caraibicae.* [**136**]

Jansson, Jan. *Tabula Magellanica.* [**A2**]

Jollain. *Nowel Amsterdam en Lamerique.* [**A6**]

Jong van Rodenburgh, Cornelius de. *Reize naar de Caribische eilanden.* [**169**]

Keye, Otto. *Het waere onderscheydt tusschen koude en warme landen.* [**94**]

Kortbondige beschryvinge van de colonie de Berbice. [**141**]

Kort en bondigh verhael. [**A17**]

Kort historisch verhaal. [**170**]

Kort verhael van Nieuw-Nederlants gelegentheit. [**99**]

Kuhn, F.A. *Beschouwing van den toestand.* [**172**]

Laet, Joannes de. *Historie ofte Iaerlijck verhael.* [**66**]

Laet, Joannes de. *Ioannis de Laet Antwerpiani Notae.* [**63**]

Laet, Joannes de. *Nieuvve wereldt.* [**37**]

Langenes, Barent. *Hand-boeck; of cort begrijp.* [**20**]

La Peyrère, Isaac de. *Drie voyagien gedaen na Groenlandt.* [**101**]

Lavaux, A. de. *Algemeene kaart van de colonie of provintie van Suriname.* [**140**]

Leubelfing, Johann von. *Ein schön lustig Reissbuch.* [**21**]

Lief-hebber. *Claar vertooch van de verradersche en vyantlijcke acten.* [**74**]

Lierzang op de verklaarde onafhanglijkheid der Noord-Amerikaansche Staaten. [**153**]

Lijkzang op het overlijden. [**A13**]

Linschoten, Jan Huygen van. *Itinerario.* [**5**]

Manifest door d'inwoonders van Parnambuco uytghegeven. [**70**]

Martens, Friedrich. *Frederik Martens nauwkeurige beschryvinge van Groenland.* [**128**]

Mercator, Gerhard. *Atlas novus.* [**56**]

Merian, Maria Sibylla. *Mariae Sibillae Merian Dissertatio.* [**132**]

Missive van bewindhebberen der Westindische Compagnie. [**149**]

Montanus, Arnoldus. *De Nieuwe en onbekende Weereld.* [**106**]

Moris, Gedeon. *Copye. Van 't journael gehouden by Gedeon Moris.* [**59**]

More excellent observations of the estate and affaires of Holland. [**31**]

Naaukeurige versameling der gedenk-waardigste zee en land-reysen. [**127**]

New York. Committee of Safety. *To the inhabitants of the colony.* [**146**]

Neyn, Pieter de. *Lust-hof der huwelyken.* [**116**]

Nieuhof, Johannes. *Gedenkweerdige Brasiliaense.* [**117**]

Nomsz, J. *Bartholomeus Las Casas.* [**157**]

Nomsz, J. *Cora, of de Peruanen.* [**156**]

Noort, Olivier van. *Beschrijvinge vande voyagie.* [**25**]

Omstandigh verhael van de Fransche rodomontade. [**107**]

Onpartydich toe-hoorder. *Brasyls schuyt-praetjen.* [**80**]

Ortelius, Abraham. *Theatrum orbis terrarum.* [**2**]

Ottsen, Hendrick. *Iournael oft Daghelijcx-register.* [**23**]

Outghersz, Jan. *Nieuwe volmaeckte beschrijvinghe.* [**9**]

Oxholm, J.N. *Bibel voor kinders.* [**171**]

Paräupába, Antonio. *Twee verscheyden remonstrantien.* [**93**]

Pertinente beschrijvinge van Guiana. [**112**]

Pertinent en waarachtig verhaal. [**122**]

Pinckard, George. *Notes on the West Indies.* [**168**]

Piso, Willem. *Historia naturalis Brasiliae.* [**79**]

Plante, Franciscus. *Francisci Plante Brugensis Mauritiados.* [**75**]

Potgieter, Barent Jansz. *Journael van 't geene vijf schepen over gekomen is.* [**102**]

Potgieter, Barent Iansz. *VVijdtloopigh verhael.* [**8**]

Practiicke van den Spaenschen aes-sack. [**43**]

Raport aan Zijne Doorluchtigste Hoogheid . . . overgegeven. [**161**]

Real Compañía Guipuzcoana de Caracas. *Manifiesto.* [**138**]

Redenen, waeromme. [**49**]

Regters, Tiebaut. *Jan Nepveu.* [**A10**]

Reys-boeck van het rijcke Brasilien. [**33**]

Roggeveen, Arent. *Le premier tome de la tourbe ardante.* [**A8**]

Romans, Bernard. *Annals of the Troubles in the Netherlands.* [**147**]

Roos, Paul François. *Eerstelingen van Surinaamsche mengelpoëzy.* [**155**]

Roos, Paul François. *Surinaamsche mengelpoëzy.* [**A16**]

Ryder, Robert. Long Iland Siruaide. [**114**]

Rym-vieren op de ieghen-woordige victorie. [**44**]

S., R. *The ballance of power.* [**A15**]

Schoppe, Sigismund van. *Copie, van den brief.* [**88**]

Schoute, H. *Gezicht van het West-Indisch-Huys.* [**162**]

Schouten, Willem Cornelisz. *Diarium vel descriptio laboriosissimi.* [**27**]

Schouten, Willem Cornelisz. *Iournal ofte beschryvinghe.* [**26**]

Schouten, Willem Cornelisz. *Iournael ofte beschryvingh.* [**81**]

Sikkena, Jan. *Nieuwe groote en seer curieuse paskaart van Geheel-Westindien.* [**137**]

Het spel van Brasilien, vergheleken by een goedt verkeer-spel. [**55**]

Spilbergen, Joris van. *Copie van een brief.* [**22**]

Spilbergen, Joris van. *t'Historiael journael.* [**24**]

Spilbergen, Joris van. *Oost ende West-Indische spiegel.* [**28**]

Spranckhuysen, Dionysius. *Triumphe van vveghen de . . . victorie.* [**45**]

Stedman, John Gabriel. *Narrative, of a five years' expedition.* [**165**]

Steendam, Jacob. *Klacht van Nieuw-Amsterdam.* [**95**]

Sterre, Dionysius van der. *Zeer aanmerkelijke reysen.* [**123**]

Steyger-praetjen, tusschen Ian Batavier en Maetroos. [**34**]

Surinam. *Reglement. Of ordre.* [**151**]

[*Surinam and Commewijne Rivers.* Manuscript map]. [**A4**]

Totius Neobelgii nova et accuratissima tabula. [**131**]

Totius Neobelgii nova et accuratissima tabula. [**139**]

Translaet uyt den Spaenschen, weghens 't gevecht. [**58**]

Treaty of Breda. *Kort en bondigh verhael.* [**A17**]

Udemans, Godefridus. *'t Geestelyck roer van 't coopmans schip.* [**61**]

United Provinces. *Copia van 't octroy . . . gegeven aan Jan Reeps.* [**121**]

United Provinces *Octroy.* [**30**]

United Provinces. *Placcaet ende ordonnantie . . . tegens Wech-loopers.* [**38**]

Usselincx, Willem. *Bedenckingen over den staet van de vereenichde Nederlanden.* [**14**]

Usselincx, Willem. *Korte onderrichtinghe ende vermaeninge.* [**32**]

Usselincx, Willem. *Naerder bedenckinghen, over de zeevaerdt.* [**15**]

Usselincx, Willem. *Vertoogh, hoe nootwendich.* [**16**]

Vanden spinnekop ende 't bieken ofte droom-ghedicht. [**17**]

Van der Kemp, Francis Adrian. *Verzameling van stukken.* [**152**]

Van der Kemp, Francis Adrian. *Lofrede op George Washington.* [**166**]

Van Santvoord, Cornelius. *Samenspraak over de Klaghte der Raritanders.* [**135**].

Veer, Gerrit de. *Vraye description de trois voyages.* [**7**]

Veer, Gerrit de. *The true and perfect description of three Voyages.* [**19**]

Vertoogh by een lief-hebber des vaderlandts vertoont. [**52**]

Vertoogh, over den toestant der West-Indische Compagnie. [**86**]

Vespucci, Amerigo. *Van der nieuwer werelt.* [**1**]

Visscher, Nicolaes. *Novi Belgii Novaeque Angliae . . . tabula.* [**87**]

Visscher, Nicolaes. *Novi Belgii Novaeque Angliae . . . tabula.* [**119**]

Voorduin, G.W.C. *Gezigten op Neerland's West-Indien, naar de natuur geteekend.* [**173**]

Vosmaer, Aernout. *Natuurkundige beschryving.* [**167**]

Vries, David Pietersz. de. *Korte historiael.* [**92**]

Vries, Simon de. *Curieuse aenmerckingen.* [**118**]

Weeklyksche Surinaamsche Courant. [**163**]

Weilburgh Plantation. [**142**]

West-Indische Compagnie. *Articulen . . . provisioneelijc beraemt.* [**50**]

West-Indische Compagnie. *Reglement byde VVest-Indische Compagnie.* [**57**]

West-Indische Compagnie. *Remonstrantie.* [**A3**]

Willemsz, Salomon. *Rapport gedaen aen Hare Ho. Mo.* [**40**]

Winter, Nicolaas Simon van. *Monzongo, of De koninglyke slaaf.* [**146**]

Wit, Frederik de. *Caerte van de rivieren van Suriname.* [**120**]

Witt, Johan de. *A discourse by Mr. De Witt concerning Surynam.* [**105**]

Zeekere vrye-voorslagen. [**103**]

Zorgdrager, C.G. *C:G: Zorgdragers bloeyende opkomst.* [**133**]

Selected Secondary Sources

Asher, G.M. *A Bibliographical and Historical Essay on the Dutch books and pamphlets relating to New Netherland and to the Dutch West-India Company and its possessions in Brazil, Angola, etc.* Amsterdam: Muller, 1854-1867.

Bachman, Van Cleaf. *Peltries or Plantations. The Economic Policies of the Dutch West India Company in New Netherland 1623-1639.* Baltimore and London: The Johns Hopkins Press, 1969.

Balmer, Randall. *A Perfect Babel of Confusion. Dutch Religion and English Culture in the Middle Colonies.* New York and Oxford: Oxford University Press, 1989.

Boogaart, Ernst van den, ed. *Johan Maurits van Nassau-Siegen 1604-1679. A Humanist Prince in Europe and Brazil. Essays on the occasion of the tercentenary of his death.* The Hague: The Johan Maurits van Nassau Stichting, 1979.

Boogaart, Ernst van den, Pieter Emmer, Peter Klein and Kees Zandvliet. *La expansión holandesa en el Atlántico.* Madrid: Mapfre, 1992.

Bosman, L. *Nieuw Amsterdam in Berbice (Guyana). De planning en bouw van een koloniale stad, 1764-1800.* Hilversum: Verloren, 1994.

Boxer, C. R. *The Dutch in Brazil 1624-1654.* Oxford: Clarendon Press, 1957.

Bubberman, F. C. et al. *Links with the past. The history of the cartography of Suriname 1500-1971.* Amsterdam: Theatrum Orbis Terrarum, 1973.

Buddingh', Bernard R. *Van Punt en Snoa. Ontstaan en groei van Willemstad, Curaçao vanaf 1634, De Willemstad tussen 1700 en 1732 en de bouwgeschiedenis van de synagoge Mikvé Israël-Emanuel 1730-1732.* 's-Hertogenbosch: Aldus Uitgevers, 1994.

Buddingh', Hans. *Geschiedenis van Suriname.* Utrecht: Het Spectrum, 1995.

Davids, C.A. *Zeewezen en wetenschap. De wetenschap en de ontwikkeling van de navigatietechniek in Nederland tussen 1585 en 1815.* Amsterdam and Dieren: De Bataafsche Leeuw, 1986.

Dillen, J.G. van. "De West-Indische Compagnie, het Calvinisme en de politiek." *Tijdschrift voor Geschiedenis* 74 (1961) 145-171.

Edelman, Hendrik. *Dutch-American Bibliography, 1693-1794.* Nieuwkoop: B. DeGraaff, 1974.

Edmundson, George. "The Dutch on the Amazon and Negro in the Seventeenth Century." *English Historical Review* XVIII (1903) 642-663.

Eekhof, A. *De Hervormde Kerk in Noord-Amerika (1624-1664).* The Hague: Martinus Nijhoff, 1913.

Emmer, P. C. "The Dutch and the Making of the Second Atlantic System," in: Barbara L. Solow ed., *Slavery and the Rise of the Atlantic System.* Cambridge: Cambridge University Press, 1991. Pp. 75-96.

Goodfriend, Joyce. *Before the Melting Pot: Society and Culture in Colonial New York City, 1664-1730.* Princeton: Princeton University Press, 1992.

Goslinga, Cornelis Ch. *The Dutch in the Caribbean and on the Wild Coast, 1580-1680.* Assen: Van Gorcum, 1971.

Goslinga, Cornelis Ch. *The Dutch in the Caribbean and in the Guianas 1680-1791.* Assen, Maastricht, and Dover, N.H.: Van Gorcum, 1985.

Heijer, Henk den. *Geschiedenis van de WIC.* Zutphen: Walburg Pers, 1994.

Israel, Jonathan I. *The Dutch Republic and the Hispanic World 1606-1661.* Oxford: Clarendon Press, 1982.

Israel, Jonathan I. *Dutch primacy in world trade 1585-1740.* Oxford: Clarendon Press, 1989.

Israel, Jonathan. *The Dutch Republic. Its Rise, Greatness, and Fall 1477-1806.* Oxford: Clarendon Press, 1995.

Jameson, J. Franklin. "Willem Usselinx, Founder of the Dutch and Swedish West India Companies." *Papers of the American Historical Association* 2 vols. New York & London: G.P. Putnam's Sons, The Knickerbocker Press, 1888.

Koeman, C. *Joan Blaeu and his Grand Atlas. Introduction to the facsimile edition of Le Grand Atlas, 1663.* Amsterdam: Theatrum Orbis Terrarum, 1970.

Klooster, Wim. "The Dutch Republic as an Economic and Political Model in Eighteenth- and Nineteenth-Century Hispanic America," in: Rosemarijn Höfte and Joke Kardux, eds. *Connecting cultures: the Netherlands in five centuries of transatlantic exchange.* Amsterdam: VU University Press, 1994. Pp. 229-237.

Koninklijke bibliotheek (Netherlands). *Catalogus van de pamfletten-verzameling berustende in de Konink-lijke bibliotheek.*

Bewertet, met aanteekeningen en een register der schrijvers voorzien, door Dr. W.P.C. Knuttel. 's Gravenhage: Algemeene landsdrukkerij, 1889-1920.

Lechner, J. "Dutch Humanists' Knowledge of America." *Itinerario* XVI no. 2 (1992) 101-113.

Ligtenberg, Catharina. *Willem Usselinx.* Ph.D. dissertation, Rijksuniversiteit Utrecht, 1914.

Mello, Evaldo Cabral de. *Olinda Restaurada. Guerra e Açúcar no Nordeste, 1630-1654.* Rio de Janeiro: Ed. Forense-Universitária, and São Paulo: Universidade de São Paulo, 1975.

Mello, José Antonio Gonsalves de. *Gente de Nação. Cristãos-novos e judeus em Pernambuco 1542-1654.* Recife: Fundação Joaquim Nabuco and Editora Massangana, 1989.

Memoire bibliographique sur les journaux des navigateurs néerlandais réimprimés dans les collections de De Bry et de Hulsius, et dans les collections hollandaises du XVII siècle, et sur les anciennes éditions hollandaises des journaux de navigateurs étrangers; la plupart en la possession de Frederick Muller. . . . Amsterdam: F. Muller, 1867.

Menkman, W.R. "Sint Eustatius' gouden tijd." *West-Indische Gids* XIV (1932-1933) 369-396.

Netscher, P.M. *Geschiedenis van de koloniën Essequebo, Demerary en Berbice, van de vestiging der Nederlanders aldaar tot op onzen tijd.* The Hague: Martinus Nijhoff, 1888.

Postma, Johannes Menne. *The Dutch in the Atlantic slave trade 1600-1815.* Cambridge: Cambridge University Press, 1990.

Price, Richard and Sally Price eds. *Stedman's Surinam. Life in an Eighteenth-Century Slave Society. An Abridged, Modernized Edition of* Narrative of a Five Years Expedition against the Revolted Negroes of Surinam *by John Gabriel Stedman.* Baltimore and London: The Johns Hopkins University Press, 1992.

Rees, O. van. *Geschiedenis der Staathuishoudkunde in Nederland tot het einde der achttiende eeuw.* 2 vols., Utrecht: Kemink en Zoon, 1865-1868.

Rink, Oliver A. *Holland on the Hudson. An Economic and Social History of Dutch New York.* Ithaca and London: Cornell University Press, Cooperstown (N.Y.): New York State Historical Association, 1986.

Rücker, Elisabeth and William T. Stearn. *Maria Sibylla Merian in Surinam.* London: Pion, 1982.

Schmidt, Benjamin. "Tyranny abroad: the Dutch Revolt and the invention of America." *De zeventiende eeuw* 11 (1995) 161-174.

Schulte Nordholt, Jan Willem. *The Dutch Republic and American Independence.* Chapel Hill & London: The University of North Carolina Press, 1982.

Sluiter, E. "Dutch-Spanish rivalry in the Caribbean Area, 1594-1609." *Hispanic American Historical Review* 28 (1948) 165-196.

Stipriaan, Alex van. *Surinaams Contrast. Roofbouw en overleven in een Caraïbische plantagekolonie 1750-1863.* Caribbean Series 13. Leiden: KITLV Uitgeverij, 1993.

Stols, Eddy. "Gens des Pays-Bas en Amérique Espagnole aux premiers siècles de la colonisation." *Bulletin de l'Institut Historique Belge de Rome* XLIV (1974) 565-599.

Swart, K.W. "The Black Legend during the Eighty Years War," in: J.S. Bromley and E.H. Kossmann, eds., *Some political mythologies: papers delivered at the fifth Anglo-Dutch historical conference.* The Hague: Nijhoff, 1975. Pp. 36-57.

Tiele, Pieter Anton. *Nederlandsche bibliographie van land- en volkenkunde.* Amsterdam: F. Muller en comp., 1884.

Vries, Jan de, and Ad van der Woude. *Nederland 1500-1815. De eerste ronde van moderne economische groei.* Amsterdam: Balans, 1995.

Warnsinck, J.C.M. *Abraham Crijnssen. De verovering van Suriname en zijn aanslag op Virginië in 1667.* Amsterdam: Noord-Hollandsche Uitgeversmaatschappij, 1936.

Whitehead, P. J. P. and M. Boeseman. *A portrait of Dutch 17th century Brazil. Animals, plants and people by the artists of Johan Maurits of Nassau.* Amsterdam, Oxford and New York: North-Holland Publishing Company, 1989.

Zandvliet, Kees. *De groote waereld in 't kleen geschildert. Nederlandse kartografie tussen de middeleeuwen en de industriële revolutie.* Alphen aan den Rijn: Canaletto, 1985.

Index